Contents

Bards in the Saddle

10th Anniversary Anthology of the
Alberta Cowboy Poetry Association

Edited by Susan Ames Vogelaar

Illustrations by Ben Crane

hancock

house

ISBN 0-88839-407-1

Cataloging in Publication Data
Bards in the saddle

ISBN 0-88839-407-1

1. Cowboys–Canada, Western–Poetry. 2. Cowboys' writings,
Canadian (English)–Canada, Western.* 3. Canadian poetry (En-
glish)–Canada, Western.* 4. Canadian poetry (English)–20th
century.* I. Vogelaar, Susan.
PS8283.C68C682 1997 C811'.54078'0352636 C97-910214-6
PR9195.35.C68C682 1997

Printed in Hong Kong—Colorcraft

Production: Sharon Boglari and Nancy Miller

Published simultaneously in Canada and the United States by

HANCOCK HOUSE PUBLISHERS LTD.
19313 Zero Avenue, Surrey, BC V4P 1M7
(604) 538-1114 Fax (604) 538-2262

HANCOCK HOUSE PUBLISHERS
1431 Harrison Avenue, Blaine, WA 98230-5005
(604) 538-1114 Fax (604) 538-2262

Foreword

Congratulations to the Alberta Cowboy Poetry Association on its 10th Anniversary. I remember back when Allan Schattle and Blaine Pickard talked about cowboy poetry around the table at our bull sale. We had never heard of such a thing, except to read the Baxter Black column in our local *Grainews*. With the help of the Pincher Creek Agricultural Society President, Susan Earl, we put together the first one-day gathering in Canada in June, 1988. From twenty poets and musicians in 1988, the gathering has grown to over 100 poets and pickers in a three-day venue.

What great memories and what a great organization. I am proud to have been a part of its beginnings.

Anne Stevick
Past President of the Alberta Cowboy Poetry Association

The earliest trappings of the Alberta Cowboy Poetry Association included the smell of manure, friends and the resulting comraderie that occurred after a bull sale along the Castle River west of Pincher Creek, Alberta.

Allan Schattle, Anne Stevick and myself got to visiting about Baxter Black and his humor and love of the western lifestyle. The conversation then turned to the cowboy poetry gathering that was occurring at Elko, Nevada. Although none of us had been to Elko, we all agreed that it sounded like a tremendous endeavor. Someone then said that a similar event should occur in Western Canada. That comment was the seed that grew into the Alberta Cowboy Poetry Association and the cowboy poetry gathering that now occurs on an annual basis. I am happy that I was there and proud to have been a part of it.

Blaine Pickard BSc, DVM
Past President of the Alberta Cowboy Poetry Association

According to dictionary definition, a cowboy is a man who looks after cattle on a ranch and does most of his work on a horse. A poem is an arrangement of lines usually with regularly repeated accent and often with rhyme. Combine these two words and you get cowboy poem. Combine the two definitions and you get; a person who looks after cattle and the arrangement of words, does most of his work on horseback with regular repeated accent often with rhyme. This is not a bad combination of English and land logic. All I know is that most everyone represented in this book is capable of working horseback and arranging words in rhyme. So feel free to lope of through the pastures this book will take you to. I know you'll enjoy and probably learn a little on the way.

Bryn Thiessen
Poet and President of the Alberta Cowboy Poetry Association

This book was a dream, a dream of a legacy of a group of poets and pickers that have formed an organization to share the values of the true western lifestyle. These poets understand the relationship with the land and value the history of those pioneers who provided the opportunity for later generations to work and live on the land. Cowboy is not a romantic hollywood image to the members of the Alberta Cowboy Poetry Association. It is a way of life that reflects family tradition and family values where life depends on the forces of nature and where neighbors care. I am honored to edit this selection of poems and songs that the writers of our association have agreed to share with the readers of our anthology. This book is our legacy. Read it, share it and enjoy.

Susan Ames Vogelaar
Poet and Editor

Alberta

A Cowboy and His Soul

Lloyd Dolen

There is nothing to compare
With the tang of autumn air
In the foothills of the Rockies
At the early wake of dawn.
Just the stillness of the night breeze
And the rustle of the leaves,
A lone calf breaks the silence
Bawling for his mom.

As I stood in awesome wonder
At the beauty there before me
And I started down the trail
Across nature's domain,
I watched a momma coyote
Leading her young family
To a place she could hunt and wander
And a home that she could claim.

Nature warned about the winter that would come and go
In the stillness of the forest and the hush of falling snow.
Like a mantle it falls in the stillness of the night,
Covering the hills and valley in a blanket of shimmering white.
Have you seen the magic display of hoar frost on the trees?
Have you felt the sting of winter in a northern arctic breeze?
Have you watched the northern lights and how they dance on high
Or watched a winter sunset light up a purple sky?

The winter beauty disappears with a warm spring breeze.
Water runs down the mountain slope and leaves adorn the trees.
The birds are singing love songs no jukebox can compare
And the fragrant smell of wild flowers flows gently in the air.
The fabric of creation can be found in nature's loom
Beneath the watchful eye of a silver smiling moon.
He watches nature's beauty as it slumbers through the night
And he watches God's creation and the night owl on his flight.

Summer days are here and you hope the time is near
To live again close to the earth and bless the land that gave you birth.
Where you can ride through the forest cool
Or sit beside some limped pool and watch a trout jump for a fly,
And see a lone cloud floating by or watch a humming bird on wing
Then you will know that you have been out where the west begins.
You've had time to ponder on how nature plays its role
In the place to live, the land God gives, to a cowboy and his soul.

Running Wild and Running Free

Lloyd Dolen

I'm going to tell a story
And most of you know why,
When the cars and tractors came along
And we bid the horse good-bye.
He brought your granddad to this land,
He plowed and went to town,
He did every job that you had to do,
And never turned you down.

He never asked what day it was
It seemed he didn't care.
All he wanted was a feed of grain
And he would do his share.
He never stopped till you said whoa
Never started till you said go,
And plodded his way every day
Through the mud or through the snow.

He played his part in making history,
He brought the cows up the trail.
He brought the doctor to your door,
And he hauled the royal mail.
He built the grade when history was made
And never let you down.
He stood by with his head held high
When the first train rolled into your town.

Progress is what they call it
When the tractor came to stay,
And cars rolled down the trail
And the horse was in the way.
He was soon forgotten
Because he ate too much feed,
He got shipped across the country
To where there was no need.

That's when history lost its image
For a different way of life.
You didn't need the horse and buggy
Not even for your wife.
It didn't take too long for her
To learn to drive a motor car.
And the horse was turned out to graze
In greener fields afar.

They were left to forage for themselves
And found water and grass to munch.
They gathered together in a band
And were called the "wild bunch."
They ran wild on the grassland,
They never had to pay no fees,
With their heads held high,
Toward a clear, blue sky,
And their tails flowing in the breeze.

If you ever saw a wild bunch
You have had the thrills
To watch the leader guard his herd,
And race across the hills.
He will hide them in a valley,
Alone he will make his stand.
You can hear him whistle loud and clear
To protect his band.

So the horse has played his role in life
No matter where you have seen.
And if you have ever seen a wild bunch
You will know what I mean
When you watch two studs fight for the band
When the grass is turning green.
So take a stand to protect the band
And please let them be.
The backbone of our history
Running wild and running free.

The Look

Bryn Thiessen

It's the look of sunlight on silver,
With the smell of frost in the air,
And the sound of a tired horse blowing
That keeps them riding out there.

It's horses jingled by starlight,
A herd held up for the cut,
The pride of the young cowboys riding,
And the warmth of the sun coming up.

For the memories are the rhymes that bring back the times,
And the places a cowboy has rode.
They seem to hang in the wind then come back again,
To warm him when he grows old.

He'll remember the friendship and laughter,
And the feel of a horse working right,
The sunsets when day's work was over,
And the sounds round the fire at night.

The sound of a good cowboy singing,
The words of the poems they said,
And the coolness of the night air he's breathing
As he lay in his old canvas bed.

For if memories are the rhymes, then he wonders of the time
When upward his soul will roam.
He stands there amazed where the star herds now graze
As he stares round his heavenly home.

For the look of sunlight on silver,
With the smell of frost in the air,
And the sound of a tired horse blowing
Will meet him when he's riding up there.

Yes, it will meet him when he's riding up there.

Victorian Verse

Bryn Thiessen

Through yonder portal shines the light;
Dawn breaking—where's gone the night?
I rise from canvas bed,
Rub my nose and scratch my head,
And listen to the eerie sounds
Of bodies rising from the ground.

O pray tell, what manner of men are these
Whose legs are bowed in parentheses?
I've come back in another time it seems;
'Tis like a bad midsummer night's dream.
So I struggle to break free.
O what fools these mortal men can be!

Then the sun rises past the hill,
And in the wind I feel a chill.
Then I awake in clammy sweat.
'Twas but a dream, yet I can't forget!
And so I take my quill in hand
To write the words I understand.

But this dream could mean my death;
For once these hands, they wrote *Macbeth*.
But now it seems they go untrue,
For I just wrote *Taming a Horse to Show*.
And my greatest love story written yet
Comes out as *Roany and a Lariat*!

So I fear that I must change my name
Lest folks should hear, think me insane.
I'll call myself Billy Rattling Lance.
And in the future should I have the chance,
I'll leave this earth as I know it
And come back down as a cowboy poet!

Spring Thaw

Rose Bibby

I went out to check the calvey cows
     in my nightgown, about three.
I weren't expectin' trouble
     and they weren't expectin' me!

So when they saw that flannel flappin'
     'round my boot tops in the breeze,
They scattered hither-thither
     wild of eye and not so pleased.

So then I waddled like a duck
     with my nightgown tucked up tight,
And tried to catch those critters
     in the beam of my flashlight.

This didn't lighten up the scene
     and the bossies were incensed.
And some took leavin' serious
     right through a barb-wire fence.

I thought I'd better stop 'em
     before they left the yard.
To cut a wider circle 'round
     I was off and runnin' hard.

My boot toe caught my nighty
     as I danced through barnyard slop.
Tripped me up and threw me down.
     I fell face first...kerplop!

I came up drippin' cow dung,
     my nightgown hung in tatters.
And now I smelled so much like them,
     my nightie didn't matter.

I tied the fence together
      then crept back to the house,
And was met upon the doorway
      by my laughin' spouse.

He held his stomach, wiped his tears,
      and rolled upon the floor.
He said, "I heard the barb-wire screech
      and was comin' out the door...

"When I saw you comin' through the yard,
      a cold, wet apparition,
Darlin' don't you think you'll scare the cows
      goin' out in that condition?"

Wishin'.....

Rose Bibby

He swaggered up the sidewalk,
 his hat pushed back on his head.
He said, "Would you get the saddle, Grandma?
 I want to practice on Old Red."

Now Red was a red paint sawhorse
 and the saddle, the smallest we had.
Just right for him to practice
 to cowboy, like his old granddad.

He'd adjust the stirrups till they almost
 came up to the soles of his boots.
Untie his rope from the tether
 and build himself a big loop.

He'd swing his rope till it whistled.
 throw it and dally up quick.
Sometimes he'd catch his grandma.
 other times, a post or a stick.

The sight of that practicing cowboy
 did this old grandma's heart good.
I'd sit there wishing and wondering
 and thinking if only I could...

Make it happen that all of his wishin'
 could come true for this little guy.
But I know only desire and practice
 bring rewards that wishin' won't buy.

Thomas, the first of five grandsons, loved to practice being a cowboy, and now, as more
of these little guys are riding Old Red, I often think that even if we could make it easier
for dreams to come true, it's really the heart and the work that goes into a dream that
makes it worthwhile in the end.

The Bachelor's Turkey

Susan Ames Vogelaar

Harold Butcher was a bachelor,
A proud and independent man.
No woman graced his kitchen,
Nor washed or wiped his pans.

He ran his cattle ranch alone
In the hills south of Pincher Creek.
He managed both ranch and home,
A woman companion he didn't seek.

Christmas season was coming
And his turkey was getting fat.
He planned a dinner for the single boys
He'd even put out the welcome mat.

When the fellows rode into the yard,
The turkey was almost done.
He made sure they were aware
He'd prepared it without anyone.

No woman's advice was needed
To cook up this magnificent feast.
He peeled and cooked the potatoes
And prepared all of the treats.

The turkey was golden and steaming.
The carving knife was sharpened with care.
Everyone gathered around
And pulled up their favorite chair.

Harold was about to prove
That women weren't needed here.
To those men waiting for dinner
That fact was certainly clear.

The first slice was juicy and tender
As it was laid upon the platter.
The second slice was placed on top,
But there was something the matter.

One of the boys saw something strange
Where the stuffing should be.
The entrails of the beast were revealed
For all of the guest to see.

There was no bread stuffing
With raisins and apples inside,
Just a bunch of intestines
With yesterday's dinner entwined.

The stench from those innards
Caused faces to turn a shade of green.
This was the strangest turkey dinner
That they had ever smelled or seen.

Harold had swore no woman was needed
To prepare and cook his meals,
But maybe he should have asked one
Cause those innards had no appeal.

That feast had lost a bit of its flavor
But the guests were somewhat kind.
They ate up the potatoes and gravy
But that turkey was put aside.

The dogs were happy that Christmas,
They had an unexpected treat.
The bachelor's turkey was sumptuous
The entrails and the rest of the meat.

Now somehow this story was leaked
To the ladies who were not there.
Seventy years later, this tale is still told
About the bachelor's Christmas fare.

Chuting the Bull

Susan Ames Vogelaar

Checking the cows on the Cowley hill,
Jake noticed the bull was looking ill.
He walked with a limp, foot rot had set in.
He had to be treated before he got too thin.

They chased him in the corral with ease,
Got ready to put him in the squeeze.
The bull took a look around that pen
And decided he'd had enough of these men.

He tossed his head and with hatred in his eyes
He cleaned out that corral chasing all the guys.
Heads were put together, they devised a plan,
Jake lost the draw so he got to be the man.

Jake was to jump right down in front of him,
Run like heck through the corral and then,
Over the pole and up the chute real quick
Hopefully before that bull got a lick!

Getting the attention of the bull wasn't tough,
He was mean and mad wanting to play rough.
With a gulp and a whew, Jake jumped right in,
That bull took one look and was right behind him.

Imagine if he'd tripped or fallen down instead,
The bull would've ripped him up, left him for dead!
Well Jake ran like heck, the bull on the attack,
Snorting with fury, thundering at his back.

A faster fellow has never been seen,
He was running ahead of his own blue jeans.
He leaped the pole and ran up the chute
Praying that log would stop that brute.

There was a resounding thud and a mighty groan,
And suddenly Jake was all alone.
His life was spared, he panted for some air.
He felt his behind, to see if it was still there.

The bull wasn't happy, he'd missed his man,
And Jake had second thoughts about that plan.
"Chuting the bull" is a catch phrase used now,
If you want to try it, ask Jake, he knows how.

Lucky Day

James Roberts

Now, Smiley was one of them guys
Who almost always had
Just one particular kind of luck;
The kind that was always bad.
He seemed to possess a quality,
A magnetism, I'd say,
That always caused the rawest deals
To be dealt his way.

Course, his disposition was such
That he never realized
That fate seemed to have it in for him
And that he was victimized.

It did not matter what went sour;
He was never in chagrin.
He'd just pick himself up and dust himself off
And give his trademark grin.

Now I'll try and give an account
To illustrate his character in full.
An event I saw with my very own ears
The pith of which is bull.

See, Smiley and me and old Bill May
Was out to check one herd
When we come upon the fateful scene
Where this event occurred.

We skirted some scrub willow
And rode a little bog
When we come out in the open,
Us and Bill May's dog.

We come upon a black baldy
Who limped as she went.
Says Billy, "Look, her off fore foot,
I think its distent."

That means swoll, y'all see,
In the words of old Bill May.
Says Smiley, "Bill, I think your right.
Let's go get her, eh."

Well, we shook out loops and jumped in pursuit
With Billy well in the lead.
And that cow, for all her gimpy appearance,
Still had a lot of speed.

Now you may wonder at our rush
Takin' that cow at a jog,
But our element of quiet surprise was ruined
By Bill May's stupid dog.

Bill, he caught her head,
And Smiley, just one heel.
And me, I never caught nothin',
I was dope man in this deal.

Now rather than tail her down
While she yet stood firmly on three,
We sought to lay a trap
And lay her down easily.

I won't go into particulars,
But I'll say to get this done
Smiley had to hold that cow
With his heel catch of one.

Billy, he let slack his rope.
That cow, she started to dig.
And Smiley, he sat arched backed
On his tiltin' rim-fire rig.

Now the cow she gave another jerk
And the saddle slipped up an inch.
And Smiley's horse just came alive
When pinched by the cinch.

The horse cut loose
And started in to pitch
With Smiley on his back screamin'
"You son-of-a-mmmm...witch!"

Words ain't important now,
His dallies bein' crossed.
Poor unlucky Smiley found
His catch couldn't be lost.

Smiley clung to his saddle
Workin' to get away.
And that cow kept a-pullin'
Neither did she want to stay,

Bill and I could not react
For like water through a sieve,
Our reason left us helpless except for this,
Something's got to give.

I s'pose some thoughts are better unthunk
As some words are better unsaid,
For in that self same moment his saddle
Went over the horse's head.

That cow feelin' her release of such
Forgot her ailment of late,
And made a high-speed beeline, Smiley in tow,
For some distant gate.

We followed as best we could
Through patches of stickers and rocks,
While Smiley flew a-skimmin' along,
His body absorbing the shocks.

All I can say is it was a sight
Whose description defies the use of words.
The cow, the rope, Smiley and saddle,
Clouds of dust and cow turds.

And then with a zing the rope come away,
The cow continued on with her quest.
And with final cartwheel and curse
Smiley and his saddle come to rest.

He looked like he'd been through a meat grinder;
His hide looked thoroughly tanned.
Yet as he struggled upright
He held something in his hand.

Says Smiley, "Boys, you'll never believe it."
He smiled in his own simple way.
"I'll be danged if it ain't a four-leaf clover.
This must be my lucky day."

Chinooks

Doris Daley

An arch of grand proportions sweeps across the western sky.
It's been rhapsodized by poets far more eloquent than I.
So fine a sight would bring a tear to Charlie Russell's eye.
Soon temps will rise and creeks will thaw and snow will liquefy.

Now I don't want to gripe about what other folks adore,
But what that arch tells me is that it's going to blow some more.
Is it windy in the foothills? Is Dolly Parton busty?
I think it's safe to say that we invented the word gusty.

Somewhere west of Granum it's another average day.
The breeze has turned the garden into vegetable puree.
The kids are putting on their ropes to go outside to play.
They lash themselves to fence posts so they will not blow away.

From Pincher Creek to Nanton all the fences are in tangles.
In Fort Macleod the folks all walk at 45-degree angles.
If suddenly the wind should stop, they'll all fall on their chins,
And the entire population will be known as Head-Smashed-Ins.

One breezy day I saddled up to check some yearling steers.
T'was fairly calm—just a few old hay bales flying past my ears.
I rode northeast, my appaloosa's rump faced west and south.
He felt the urge and raised his tail, and the bit flew outta his mouth.

Now, Alberta doesn't need hot air a-blowin' in the south.
There's lots of that in Edmonton when Ralphie wags his mouth.
There's some who say the premier isn't worth a bag of oats.
But I've a grand suggestion that will win him tons of votes.
Why can't he spend our taxes on some scientific books,
And figure out a way to take the blow out of Chinooks!

On the Dash or Behind the Seat

Doris Daley

"Darlin," I said in my sweetest voice,
Trying hard not to show my distress.
"You haven't by chance seen a matchbook around
Where I wrote that horse trader's address?"

She cocked up an eyebrow and shot me a look
That implied I was not Mr. Neat.
"No, I haven't," she said, "but you might start the search
On the dash or behind the seat."

"It's not on the fridge?" I desperately asked,
"The junk drawer? The dining room table?"
"Don't think so," she smiled. Then panic set in.
I felt dizzy and weak and unstable.

"Botheration!" I cried. "Shucky darns and oh heck!"
Or words to that general effect.
Then headed outside to the old 4 x 4
Knowing my morning was wrecked.

It was built Ford tough, with plenty of gump
To charge through the mud like a brute.
The paint had held up, just the odd nick or two,
But the inside looked more like Beirut.

Look on the dash, my darlin' had said.
It was cluttered and choked like a bog.
The matchbook stayed hid, but I found a jar lid
And the missing King Rope catalog.

My check book was there, and so were my spurs,
And some wrenches I thought I should have.
My old fencin' pliers and Home Hardware fliers,
Plus an old can of Franklin Teat Salve.

I mined that occasion for all it was worth
And finally admitted defeat.
Then girding my loins and steeling my nerve
I turned to the back of the seat.

My bullwhip I spied, and under my slicker
Were feedbags, a glove and the brand book.
And the pain in my knee was a sure sign to me
That I'd finally found the old hay hook.

But matches? No luck. I might've as well hunted
For emeralds or kangaroo tails.
I got all the floor, banged my head on the door
And knocked over a can full of nails.

I know when I'm licked, so slunk back inside,
Frustration was etched on my face.
My sweet little wife saw my pain and my strife
And gave me a soothing embrace.

We kissed and we smooched. She gave me a hug.
I fingered her gold heart-shaped locket
Then she lovingly patted my head and exclaimed,
"Why, the matches are here in your hip pocket!"

The Great March West

W. J. "Robbie" Robertson

They called us the North West Mounted Police,
We came west when the west was young.
In the summer of eighteen seventy-four,
Our work had just begun.

We had come from every walk of life
To seek adventure in the vast northwest.
Farmers and soldiers and school boys,
Canadian youth at its best.

We had spent the winter in Winnipeg,
Where we learned to shoot and ride.
From Sergeant Major, Big Sam Steele,
We first learned Mountie pride.

Sam Steele was a tough young son of a gun
Who took everything in stride.
But when the weather was worse than thirty below
We didn't have to ride.

He shaped us up for that marathon trek
Which was known as the Great March West.
And would take us from Fort Dufferin
To the hub of that hornet's nest.

Where whiskey and killing were rampant
At a place called Fort Whoop-Up.
And Canadian Indians were being plagued
In their very own Wickiup.

The Great March West, a magnificent sight,
Saw three hundred mounted men
In troops of bays and grays and blacks,
But it was not just equestrian.

There were teams of horses, and beef on the hoof,
And following in behind
Was a string of oxen with Red River carts.
You could see the parade wind

Its way across the prairie,
In a colorful array.
Red-coated young adventurers
Making twenty miles a day.

The first outlaws were soon routed,
And respect of the Natives gained.
But the Red Coats still had a job to do,
So on the Prairies we remained.

We were here when the mighty Crowfoot,
Chief of the Blackfoot Nation,
Told Sitting Bull to leave us alone
Or face Blackfoot retaliation.

The railway, as promised, soon rolled west
Across the open plain,
And brought a rush of settlers,
But we were here to keep it tame.

From the edge of Upper Canada,
Far west to the Great Divide,
Sprawled the Northwest Territories
One thousand miles wide.

And from those Territories
Came the provinces three,
Manitoba, Saskatchewan and Alberta,
Homes for people who longed to be free.

To pursue the dream of happiness
In a place they could call their own.
And put down roots in that prairie sod,
And never have to roam.

We served with French and then McLeod,
As leaders of the Force.
Loyalty, bravery, valor and pride
Were just a matter of course.

The legendary Jerry Potts
Became a member of our band.
The bow-legged little Metis scout
Helped us find our way 'round the land.

There was Allen, who unhorsed Sitting Bull,
And McDonald, who took his gun,
When the Sioux had come north of the Medicine Line
And out-numbered us twenty to one.

Oh, there were many living legends
In those first three hundred men,
And we'd ride with them to the gates of hell
And ride right back again.

When times got tough and we wanted to quit,
We'd think of big Sam Steele.
For the pride and the bravery he'd instilled
Was something very real.

And we knew if we could carry on,
A heritage we'd bequeath
To those who followed after us,
When our bones were laid beneath

The sod we had protected
In the days of the wild frontier.
When we'd first promised to "Maintain the Right"
Without favor, affection or fear.

They called us the North West Mounted Police.
We came west when the west was young.
But a hundred and twenty years later
Our work is still not done.

Cowboy Poetry

W. J. "Robbie" Robertson

It goes right back to the days of yore,
A hundred years ago or more.

Cowboys sittin' round a fire
When Hank says, "Bill, I know you're a liar,

"But tell me that tale 'bout the wild cayuse
You rode with one hand while stuffin' snoose

"Plumb under your lip with the other hand
As he bucked so hard, he shook off his brand.

"But you rode him till he came to a dead stand still.
Won't you tell me that story again, please Bill?"

But Tom said, "Bill, I'm gonna yell
If once more I hear that yarn you tell.

"I'll get so mad, I'll go back home,
Why don't you put it into a po'm?"

And so Bill did before next morn'
And that's how cowboy poetry was born.

Grampa's Saddle

Dixie Lee White

See that old saddle up there on the rail?
If it could talk, it would tell you a tale
Of riders it's known and those that were thrown,
Of wranglers and rustlers and strawberry roans.

It's held some tiny cowboys riding tandem with their dad,
And known more than a horse or two that surely were plumb bad.
It carried Grampa Charlie home when his heart gave out that day,
And Becky to her wedding on the 25th of May.

It's been witness to more cowboys riding rough stock than we know.
Used by pick-up men a plenty at the local rodeo.
Carried new calves through the storm when ol' winter wouldn't quit,
And lovers of a moonlight ride just for the pleasure of it.

The leather now is dark with age and patched and worn it's true.
A rider it won't hold again, that saddle's paid its due.
Still, it rests there paying homage to a wondrous history
Of the ranch lands of Alberta and the cowboy legacy.

Cowboy Logic

Dixie Lee White

You've heard of cowboy logic,
Seems to me it's true.
A cowboy says just what he thinks,
And he expects the same of you.

He doesn't want that double talk
Or fancy words and phrases.
Just chew it fine and spit it out
And don't be hesitatin'.

A cowboy's word is good as gold,
Or was in days long past.
I'd like to think its still the same
That their promises'll hold fast.

If a cowboy has a problem,
Well, there won't be great debate.
He'll check his odds, cut his losses,
And in seconds a decision he'll make.

Most cowboys aren't much for far-range plans,
Or for dwellin' for long in the past.
They work, love and play and live each day
Just like it was their last.

When a cowboy sits round the fire with the boys,
It's tale-tellin' time and the cards are in hand.
He may get to drinkin' and makin' some noise,
that's just pure fun...cowboy brand.

When the sun sinks low in the Porcupines,
And your cowboy sits weary in saddle,
And it seems too much like an uphill climb,
Some days just too much of a battle,

I'll bet he looks out on the range land
As the sun sinks low in the west,
And tips his hat to the "man upstairs"
Cause he knows they're both doin' their best

Stampede

(Song)

Don Brestler

Way down on the Cimarron, out on the Chaparral,
Three thousand longhorns on the northern trail,
Hot, dusty days for a thousand miles.
Take them easy boys, they're spooky and they're wild.

On the trail in June of 1884,
Texas to Montana for the matador,
Ten mounted riders, good men every one.
God help us all if these critters run.
(Repeat chorus: Stampede, Stampede)

The air was still that evening when they bedded down.
The riders sang softly as they rode around.
The others slept with their night horse tied.
It could be tonight when every man must ride.

It was much too quiet, all was not well.
Then came a rumble from the distant hill.
A far off flash lit up the sky.
Brave men pray, sometimes brave men die.
(Chorus)

One bit steer arose to sniff in the air.
The rumble grew closer, fear was everywhere.
The night grew dark and hope grew dim.
A restless herd, soon it would begin.

All at once it happened, oh so very fast.
The thunder and the lightening, such a terrible crash.
Twelve thousand hooves then shook the ground.
Ride cowboy ride, the stampede is on.
(Chorus)

In the pouring rain, into the dark of night,
Following the herd as fast as they could ride.
Into the lead rode a bold young man.
Turn the herd around, cowboy, if you can.

We finally got them milling at the break of day.
With the big run over they settled down to stay.
Missing the kid that rode ahead,
His horse fell, the young cowboy lay dead.
(Chorus)

We buried them there, in trust to the Lord,
And wrote these words on his grave-head board.
"If heaven has grass and longhorn cows
And needs a hand, it's got a good one now."

I have been a cowboy all my doggone life.
If anything scares me in the dead of night,
It is to hear the pounding of a thousand feet
And hear the cry, the night cry of stampede.
(Chorus)

Desperado (Ballad of Ed Dalton)
(Song)
Don Brestler

Through the grasslands of Montana
He trailed a small herd north.
There was a different brand
On nearly every horse.

Well dressed and well mounted,
A six gun on each hip,
A young, good-looking man,
Tall, trim and very quick.

Stopped by the sheriff
Somewhere along the way.
They both knew the score,
Their guns came into play.

The sheriff then went down,
A bullet in his chest.
Before he hit the ground
He grazed the outlaw's neck.

(Chorus)
Desperado, desperado
From Montana came.
Ed Dalton was his name.

He now rode like the wind,
North across the line.
Refuge he would need
For a certain length of time.

A big silk bandanna
Covered his ugly scar.
No one asked him questions,
This stranger from afar.

He broke many horses
For ranchers all around.
A better hand and rider
Just nowhere could be found.

His horse was always saddled
In the barn each night.
A short way from the bunkhouse
In case he had to ride.
(Chorus)

A gun beneath his pillow,
The other above the door,
They wouldn't take this cowboy
Without his forty-four.

He fell in love with Winnie,
A girl from Twin Butte.
His past he could not change,
This gunman on the loose.

When the Mounties found him,
Freedom was not his.
Winnie brought him food
To his lookout on the ridge.

He gave her his best horse,
A token of his love,
Then on a moonlight night
He once again rode south.
(Chorus)

But a few years later
On a bar room floor
Lay the handsome stranger,
The outlaw rides no more.

He lived by the six-gun,
He died the same way.

Why the man went bad
Is really hard to say.

Cowboys and campfires,
Stories to be told,
The hills hold the secret
From the early days of old.

The wind whispers softly,
The night shadow's long.
A rider on the ridge,
The legend still lives on.
(Chorus)

The King

Tom G. Hogarth

We were camped at night on Mosquito Creek.
It was dusk, the campfire coals glowed red.
The wrangler shifted the chew in his cheek
With a look so strange, this is what he said.

"Boys, there's a bad black stud horse,
He's a-running those hills tonight.
You'll see him away up on the ridges
Outlined by the morning's early light.

"The sun rays shine upon his brands;
Brands that marked him from the start.
The one place man hasn't marked him
Is there, in the middle of his heart.

"He is the spirit of the cowboy,
Spirit of the West, maybe the wind.
Much too long since he felt a rope,
Far too much spirit left to bend.

"Unlike the men who hate him so
And would try to bring him down,
He will remain unfettered and unbowed
Cherishing freedom to own his ground.

"And he will run you until tomorrow,
Or he will run you until he dies.
A good mount under you and God's own luck,
You might see that light in his eyes.

"He is old and maybe he's even ancient.
It's all there running in his blood.
He is a rogue and he is a renegade,
Luring away prized mares to his brood.

"So when the mist is out there on the breaks
And the dew drops on the fern frond shines,
He will wade his way through the marshes
And he will melt away into the pines.

"In my dreams I see him like a vision.
I don't know if I'm him or he is me,
Trying valiantly to avoid the capture
Or trying just as hard to break free.

"So if you want you call him accursed,
Call him outlaw, call him anything.
He covers his mares; a lot of ground
Though battle scarred, call him KING."

Farmer Sam

Irene E. Wert

Sam was a real happy farmer
With a good wife, three sons and a daughter.
Sam figured his life would be perfect
If only his farm had more water.
One year just as spring turned to summer
A new road was built by his place.
When the crew said, "We'll make you a dugout,"
That sure put a smile on Sam's face.
With the government's finest equipment
They dug a hose, ninety by thirty.
The kids swam, the cows drank, the cistern got filled,
And Sam's vehicles never went dirty.
Then one day, well into October,
In the late afternoon, about four,
A big flock of ducks flew onto Sam's farm,
And then more and then more and then more.
When they'd all settled down in the evening,
That dugout was ducks, wall to wall.
Sam said he was glad they could use it.
He didn't begrudge them at all.
Well, a heavy frost came toward morning.
Didn't favor good Sam one iota.
Those damn ducks flew off with a blanket of ice.
Now Sam's dugout is in South Dakota.

One for Peggy

Irene E. Wert

Peggy smiled as she stood by her window sill
And gazed at her garden, the trees and the hill.
Enjoying the morning in all of its charm,
And thanking the Lord that she lived on a farm.
Old Jake broke the spell of the beautiful morn,
Tore up the road, barking up a storm.
A white cadillac turned into the lane,
And the driver got out saying, "Let me explain.
I was driving, perhaps a trifle too fast,
When your rooster appeared on the road, alas.
I slammed on the brakes, but to no avail.
Your rooster's as dead as an old doornail."
Peg was sad at the thought of her rooster dyin',
But as farmers know, there is no use cryin'.
So before she could tell him it didn't matter,
The stranger once more began to chatter.
"I'm ever so sorry, I want to be fair.
Please let me replace your rooster there."
Peggy said, "Well, I don't want to fight ya.
There are the hens and I hope they like ya!"

Hay Time Horses

Buddy Gale

They ran on the range
Ten months of the year.
Only part broke,
Very hard to get near.

Cowboys never had time
To start them out slow.
It was hook to the mower
And know you will go.

Where will you go,
You never do know.
The only thing certain
Is it won't be too slow.

If you think riding broncs
Takes lots of skill,
Try a seat on a mower
Flying over the hill.

If you've never been there
It's hard to explain.
But these horses ran faster
Than a runaway train.

You sit there and pull hard
With all of your might,
And hope all the big rocks
Stay down out of sight.

Your ride is a fast one
And you hope you can last,
Till they run out of wind
As the world rushes past.

I would have to say hay time
Was like going to war.
You usually were banged up
And your seat was real sore.

For flying the three miles
From the barn to the range
Is only the beginning
Of things that will change.

There's dropping the sickle
When it's time to cut grass.
Here's where the teamsters
Land flat on their back!

They drag along,
Hardly touching the ground,
Hoping to hold on
Till the horses slow down.

There's pieces of hay time
That will never appear,
Lost by runaway horses
As they ran wild with fear.

I think when you look up
At the stars in the sky,
And you see that star falling
As it flashes on by...

Then you look at it closer
And your face starts to frown.
It's just an old mower team
Trying hard to slow down.

Chilcotin Cowboy

Buddy Gale

Pull up a chair,
I'll tell you a story
Of a young cowboy
From the hills west of town.

He was breaking green horses,
And doing a good job,
For a rancher who thought
He was the best hand around.

He knew from years
Of looking at cowboys
That the kid was as cool
As the ice in your glass.

His dad was a man
Who had been a sheriff.
They lived up the valley
In the Chilcotin Pass.

He taught the young cowboy
How to break horses,
And do the border shift
When he made the fast draw.

He knew from years
Of facing fast gunmen
That the boy was
The quickest that he ever saw.

The rancher was losing
To rustlers and outlaws.
They shot up his foreman
The last time in town.

He knew he could use
Some hard rock young cowboys,
But he didn't know where
They were to be found.

He pulled up his horse
And called the young cowboy.
Those riders we see
Have no business here.

They said to the rancher,
"We are tired of traveling.
So we'll drop off our packs
And unload our gear."

The young cowboy said,
Quiet and deadly,
"You might stay longer
Than anyone planned.

"Though four out of seven
Won't make it even,
I think I'll need three
For the digging at hand."

He then drew his guns
In the flick of an eyelash.
And they knew they were lucky
They had now pushed his hand.

Now the rancher rides easy
In a world full of sunshine,
As he watched the pony
Walk along slow.

For his daughter married
The bronc-riding cowboy.
And his grandson is telling
The wild horse to go.

Dad's Out Sortin' Cattle

Morrie MacIntosh Goetjen

Now sortin' cows at our ranch
Was an ordeal, there's no doubt.
Whether it was cuttin' culls from keepers
Or sortin' lame ones out.

And it didn't matter what I knew
Or the knowledge that I had,
There was one boss in our corral
And that was dear old dad.

You see, dad, he knew all the cows,
Their history to a "T."
He knew the dam, he knew the sire,
The whole damn pedigree.

He knew the ones to watch out for,
And the ones that crawled the fence.
And he gave his orders, loud and clear,
Though they made such little sense.

Like, "Hey, you fool! Watch that gate!
Now let her have her head!
No! No! Dang-blammit, not that gate!
The one 'long side the shed!

"You're movin' 'em away too slow.
Can you go a little faster?
Now hustle up and head 'em off!
And now you've gone on past 'er!

"Oh! There she is, right in front!
Standin' by the gate!
Now come around and haze her in.
Geez, hurry, don't be late!

"Now, walk behind her nice 'n slow.
By golly! There's her calf!
Take the pair, if you can.
No point in takin' half!

"Well, do your best to get 'em all,
At least a matchin' set!
And there's that lame one from last spring!
She's open now, I'll bet!

"No! No! Golldarnitall!
Take a look at where I point!
It's that white-faced cow that's got the limp,
And I'm sure it's her stifle-joint!"

Well, the air turned blue sortin' cows.
It was dad's familiar tune.
Young or old, seasoned or green,
No one was immune.

He'd roar his orders above the noise.
And his swear words, they were varied.
You might think that I'm lyin' to ya,
But his voice has always carried.

Well, then one day a silence fell
Upon our old corral,
And the cows were quiet and the music dropped
As did our own moral.

See, dad was called away beyond
To that rangeland up across.
But I have no doubt, he just took over
And made himself the boss.

I can hear his shoutin' oh so loud,
"St. Peter, watch that gate."
And, "Get behind that snotty cow,
Geez, hurry, don't be late!

"You're movin' 'em away too quick!
You'll startle 'em sure as heck!
We'll have cows a bustin' fences,
And we're sure to have a wreck!

"And use that gate to head 'em off,
And slam it hard!" he'd vow.
"And knock off some of them pearly things
'Cuz they're scaring all the cows!"

Well, I'll never know if St. Pete
Is good at takin' orders.
But if he lets my dad run the show,
Dad'll roar at all the sorters.

But you know my dad and ol' St. Pete,
They're really bound to clash.
And dad will roar like thunder,
And St. Pete a lightnin' flash.

Well, there is no doubt that dad's the boss
Where men and cows do battle,
'Cuz every time the thunder roars
I know dad's sortin' cattle.

A Day on the Trail

B. J. Smith

We gathered up the children,
Rode Kananaskis way.
It was completely natural,
Not like it is today.

Have you wasted a day or lost it?
Was it well or sorely spent?
Just have a day upon the trail
And learn to be content.

The wonders of the back country,
Mother Nature's handiwork.
Setting up the first camp,
Not a child did shirk.

Can you see the sun is setting?
The day is slipping fast.
Kids settlin' in and talking of
The grizzly that we passed.

You can hear their hearts rejoicing
As they snuggle into bed.
As the light is fading,
I can't help but bow my head.

As the mountain guards our slumber,
I think that God will say,
You have earned one more tomorrow,
By the trail you rode today.

Magpie Tales

Rob Osberg

Away back then, or so I've been told,
The magpie was there to watch it unfold.
From a cottonwood tree he surveyed the change.
Silently, he watched the demise of free range.

On a bison he sat as the herd roamed the plain.
Oceans of grass swayed in the wind and the rain.
The buffalo could travel for days and not stop.
There was no limit to the grass they could crop.

Then amid the smell of black powder and death,
The great herd of buffalo breathed its last breath.
And the magpie was there to pick the bones clean,
Only remnants of the herd were left to be seen.

The ranchers came west for land almost free.
The magpie saw cattle from his cottonwood tree.
The grasslands still reached to where the land met the sky,
And he knew it would end, but he knew not why.

Farmers arrived and with them brought barb wire,
To fence out the cattle and grow grain was their desire.
Soon acres of wheat covered the vast prairie,
And a tangle of barbs was the fate for the unwary.

Where others have vanished, the magpie lives on.
He thrives in the new when the old is all gone.
He's wily and sassy because he saw it all change,
From the cottonwood he saw the end of free range.

No longer can herds roam the wide-open plain.
Barb wire was stretched and the wild West was tamed.
For the sake of good order an old freedom was shorn,
And a new breed of fence-mending cowboy was born.

Fears

Rob Osberg

The sun was setting when he finally reached the lineshack.
It cast sinister shadows over the valley far below.
By the time the horse was stabled, snow pelted his back,
And the pines twisted erratically as the wind began to blow.

The storm hit with full force before his supper was put away,
Before the glow of the barrel stove had warmed his butt.
The wind howled through the eaves as night succeeded day.
It moaned down the chimney, putting a lonely ache in his gut.

He hitched his chair closer to the blasting heat,
And poured himself a whiskey in a thumb-smudged tin.
His shoulders sagged in weary forlorn defeat,
As he asked himself, "What have I done and where have I been?"

He came close to tears as he thought of all those years
Wasted in bars thinking life was just a lark.
And the foreboding fears whispered in his ears
Of the little time left to make his mark.

Thoughts of warm pretty women teased his mind,
And he wondered why he had never taken a wife.
Images of laughing children were all he could find
As he struggled to think of the real meaning of life.

He thought of the home that he'd never owned,
And the constant moving from pillar to post.
Living alone was the only life he had known,
But he was tired and love was what he wanted most.

The clatter of a dish knocked down by a packrat startled him,
And he laughed loudly to chase the lonely thought away.
But the wind moaned down the chimney again,
So he poured another drink, put in a log and waited for the light of day.

The Diamond and a Half Mare

Wendy Vaughan

Dad had run some wild horses in
Off the hills of the Old Bar Cee.
And among the lot was an old black mare,
Well aged it was plain to see.

Her wither was sharp and high
And her muzzle was silvery gray.
And her back dipping low
Showed well her years in its sway.

Her mane was long and tangled
Her tail near drug the ground,
Her ribs and hip bones were protruding,
She'd wintered hard when found.

Her left hip was well marked
With the diamond and a half brand,
An iron not used in twenty years
By either the owner or his hands.

Her back and rump were mottled
With the gray of sucking ticks,
And her hooves were broken and ragged
Where the rocks had got their licks.

But her eyes, so keen and sharp,
Watched our every move.
And her ears flicked back and forth
While the young stuff milled a groove.

We cut away the young slicks,
Then ran her in the chute.
Dad pulled her mane and tail while Doug and I
Snapped ticks on the gate planks with our boots.

She never fought the chute,
Just stood while we picked off ticks,
Though her nostrils would flare and she'd snort
If we moved a little too quick.

We turned her back in the corral,
Leaving her there for the day.
In the morning when the three of us rode out
The old mare led the way.

She passed us on the trail
As we rode to the river and hills
Waited for us at the north gate
While dad opened it, she stood impatiently still.

Then she trotted through and led on
Up the range to the river bank,
And down the short-cut trail steep incline
Then sniffed the running water, but never drank.

We sat and watched as she crossed the Ghost
On the way to her hills she was free.
She never paused or looked back as she trotted
Up the draw, and disappeared in the trees.

Well, we never saw her again,
But while riding the river the next spring
I saw the bald eagles circling high in the hills
And these thoughts in my mind took wing;

Were they circling some carrion they'd found.
Could it be the old mare had cashed in?
And did her spirit now soar as free as an eagle
On the warm, spring Chinook wind?

Runaway to Ontario

Darryl Vance

Working on a stockyard crew
We're the night shift boys through and through.
We brand and needle the calves all right.
We bed and feed and load the train at night.

After midnight we were told
The east-bound train was on hold.
We move the car by brake and hand
And load the calves, and then they stand.

We spot the car before the main line
And set the brake, it's going fine.
One more turn on the brake,
The car lets loose for heaven's sake!

Louie and Verle grab some railway ties
To put in front of the wheels alright.
It chops them up, just like match sticks.
The boys shout Jump! before we hit the ditch.

The car jumps onto the railway track,
A runaway car there's no looking back.
We chase the car until we're out of breath,
A runaway car and we're scared to death.

They clocked the car going a hundred clicks
Through Fort Macleod, what will it miss?
It finally stopped with no calves down,
About ten miles west of Lethbridge town.

Sixteen wheels on a cattle car,
Fifty-two calves, are they going far?

Brand Inspectors

Darryl Vance

I got a call last winter,
From a farmer on the flat,
To impound some livestock...
The damage, it was bad.

I traveled to the farmer's place
And there, much to my surprise,
Rooted nine hungry hogs,
Humongous was their size.

I conferred with Clint and Chuck
What we should do to lock them up.
For we know it's very hard
To load and haul them to the yards.

The farmer's wife thought we were nuts,
Such a difficult job, that's not much.
"See in my yard where they dig?
Please get rid of these pigs!"

We rounded up some panels.
Clint got his truck and trailer.
Chuck brought his horse and rope.
The farmer's wife got paler.

I brought a sack of grain
And put up all the panels.
Three extra helpers came,
We referred to the inspector's manual.

The pigs were locked in the panels,
We lured them with the grain.
The farmer's wife came by to help
She put us all to shame.

She raced in behind the hogs,
Boy were they surprised.
The hogs all jumped in the truck
When they heard the woman's cries.

The saga of this tale,
Be it truth or fun,
Just leave it to a woman
And we'll know the job is done.

Hummingbird Homesick Blues
(Song)
Christine C. Schauer

Last night I watched the sun go down on a rocky western slope,
Where only just a year ago my horse and I did lope.
And I long to be back there again and ride across those hills,
To forget the day-to-day routine of work and rent and bills.

(Chorus)
The Hummingbird is calling me, as it runs on endlessly,
From the mountain peaks to the valley below,
Through the jack pines and the diamond willow,
My heart can hear the call, my heart can hear the call.

Back here in the rat race, where the rats are in the lead,
Some peaceful, untamed beauty is really what I need.
The time to smell the roses and discover who I am,
In relation to the universe and to my fellow man.
(Chorus)

There is no greater feeling than to breathe that mountain air.
To be at one with nature, like the deer and the elk and bear.
The creek they call the Hummingbird is more like home to me,
More than any place that human hands can make will ever be.

The Hummingbird is calling me, as it runs on endlessly,
From the mountain peaks to the valley below,
Through the jack pines and the diamond willow,
My heart can hear the call, my heart can here the call.
Oh, can't you hear the call...

10

Christine C. Schauer

The rider was so nervous, fear was in her voice.
"If I'm ever going to ride again, I really have no choice."
Unpleasant memories flooding back of runaways and wrecks,
"Will this be any different, am I about to break my neck?"

The rider's heart was pounding as she gathered up the lines.
One foot in the stirrup, boy, she'd tried this many times.
The pony stood there patiently, as patient ponies do,
As if to softly whisper, "Relax, I'll take good care of you."

The pony kept her promise and the rest is history.
She redefined with confidence how this riding thing should be.
She'd go along so willingly, no need for whip or spur,
Your age or your experience didn't matter much to her.

No show-like conformation, she didn't have a lot of size.
But a million-dollar attitude with a kind and gentle eye.
She's too round at the wither and a little high at the hip.
A little ponchie in the middle, cinch up tight...or it'll slip.

There aren't too many like her, she's a special kind of horse,
And if tragedy is gonna strike, it'll be one like that of course.
The sixteenth day of August, in 1994,
Found her in a world of hurt, no need to tell you more.

Don't really know what happened, I guess we never will.
We won't jump to no conclusions, we'll just have to wait until...
The vet said, "Near as I can tell, I'd have to say it's broke."
It just can't be, say it ain't so. Please tell me it's a joke.

The pony nickered softly, not a lot that we can do.
"Relax," I whispered weakly, "I'll take good care of you."
Kept her as comfortable as possible, really didn't look too good.
Just had to get it x-rayed, we'd do everything we could.

Her pasture mates were lined up as if to say good-bye.
They somehow seemed to know that this would be her last ride.
She hopped into the trailer just like every time before.
On three good legs she trembled, as I slowly closed the door.

The others ran beside us, tried to beat us to the gate,
Calling, "Please, don't take her from us...no...please...wait..."
I can still hear them calling as we pulled on down the lane.
I tried to fight it, but they knew, she'd not be back again.

The x-rays they confirmed what we already knew,
The bone was shattered beyond repair, only one thing we could do.
"We thank you for your kind concern, your understanding way,
All good things come to an end, and this one is today."

Again she was so nervous, fear was in her voice.
"Oh, I am so very sorry...I really have no choice.
If horses go to heaven, if there's a place for her up there,
The wrangler whispers softly, "Relax, I'll see she's in good care."

Tribute to Barney

Bill Wearmouth

How or why Barney arrived, I don't recall.
A nice bay gelding about fourteen and a half hands tall.
Not much lineage to be proud of in his past.
Maybe a bit of thoroughbred made him think he was fast.

And some clydesdale, you could tell by the hair on his feet.
But his sire was probably quarterhorse, that made him worth his keep.
Well everyone was busy and Barney never got broke till he was nearly four.
To bother with that outcast was just another chore.

Then brother Dick rode him for a while, but as things go,
Dick broke a leg and Barney went out to pasture for another year or so.
By now he was six, and while he was willing and smart,
He should have been a rodeo horse had he been trained right from the start.

But he become a school pony, winter, spring and fall,
And in between took his turn hitched to a wagon or a plow.
At one time or another he bucked us all off,
But he never refused a challenge, and at that you couldn't scoff.

Next we took Barney to some local gymkannas in the spring.
Not racing, but as usual Barney would do most anything.
At bareback wrestling he was steady as a rock,
And in steeplechase he was really quite a shock.

He wasn't used to jumping those three-foot fences
And cleared them by another three feet, wasn't taking any chances.
Well next thing you know, of all his varied deeds,
He followed the chuck wagons at the Calgary Stampede.

And we were never late once, though he wasn't so fast.
We got out with the wagon and didn't have to make it up on the home-stretch dash.
Through the mud and the dust and the wrecks and the rain
Nothing fizzled Barney, he proved it again and again.

But finally I got riding for faster rigs, stepped up the pace.
All the wagon horses were now thoroughbreds trying to win the big race.
So once again Barney went out to pasture and to get fat,
But his adventures weren't over, his life wasn't like that.

It was early November, hunting time in the hills out west.
Brother Dennis and friend Bob Turner headed out to try their best.
They were heading up the Panther to look for some deer.
Just those two on foot with Barney packing the gear.

Well, when you hunt the Panther, as all of you hunters know,
You gotta cross it seven times, if it's upstream you go.
Now Barney had never been in the bush, but that makes this story more fun.
A hundred-pound pack, now add two hunters and their guns.

Over four hundred pounds to swim that swollen river with all of that pack.
Now add a deer and swim it seven times again coming back.
He got used to the mountains and overloaded packs.
Once he carried three hundred pounds of moose twelve miles back.

Of course Barney was getting older now, sometimes took the kids for a ride.
But I'm glad to tell you the last years were easy on that tough old hide.
No more races, no chuck wagons or rivers to swim.
He just roamed the big pasture and grazed at his whim.

The end finally came and he went peacefully one night.
And sometimes fond memories of Barney come back, it seems only right.
Now maybe animals are inferior creatures as the Bible would have us understand,
But I can't think of Barney as much less than a man.

Queen of the Hills Ranch

Alanna Murray

Did you ever need a break;
A place to get away?
A place real quiet
Where you could just go and pray.

I found a beautiful spot
Like that today.
Trees, a river and a bank
Just to sit.

Isn't it wonderful how God's creation
Can make you forget your troubles and sorrows,
And help you look forward
To better tomorrows.

Just when you're down,
And feeling all alone,
That's when God picks you up
And carries you home.

He shows you His world
And how great it can be.
And how lucky you are to be here,
And be free.

Sitting on the banks
Of that rushing little river,
A soft breeze blew
And sent through me a shiver.

A whisper from God to say,
Look at what you've got.
I started counting my blessings
Right there on the spot!

Real Cowboy

Leane Buxton

I'll wear a long-sleeved shirt
and a pair of Wrangler jeans.
I'll tell some wild stories
of the places I have been.

I'll learn to be a poet
of extraordinary flair.
I'll ride upon the prairies
for the cities I don't care.

I'll be in every rodeo
that comes into our town.
I'll ride the bucking bronco,
ain't cut out to be the clown.

I want to follow in his footsteps
once I'm finished with my toys.
And be just like my grandpa,
going to be a real cowboy.

Rocky Mountain Home

Leane Buxton

He was born in the Rocky Mountains
In an old coal-mining town.
It's all but gone now
Since the mines shut down.

He lives now upon the prairies,
And a rancher he's become.
He tells some wild tales
Of the place that he came from.

But it's the cowboy and his horse
And the woman by his side,
And four hundred red baldies
That have become his pride.

Still he dreams of snow-capped mountains,
Of valleys and rock creeks,
Of wildlife and trails,
And wind biting at his cheeks...

Of a cabin and a good horse
And no roads for miles around,
And a snag in the river
Where a bull trout can be found.

He yearns to journey back,
With his horse he wants to roam.
To breath that mountain air
Because the Rockies are his home.

At the Rancher's Corral

Ezra E. Eberhart

At the rancher's corral I stood one day,
Had just wandered by like an unbranded stray.
The smell of smoking hair from the branding iron's sear
Told the whole story of why this crew was here.

For the way things were proceeding my life surely did impress.
The way your sons and daughters kept up with all the rest.
While cowboys on their ponies drug those calves to a branding fire,
Teenage boys and girls did the wrestling in cowboy-style attire.

While some did the branding, others made two sharp cuts.
And the very young picked prairie oysters and put them in their pots.
Someone took the horns off, others gave vaccine shots,
Before the little critter was turned loose to mother up.

Then when the work was finished and a coffee break was near,
The young who'd done the wrestling left the corral in high gear.
To the water trough for a scrubbing, then maybe even a cool beer,
Walking up to the smallest lad to shake his hand so dear.

For when I slowly spoke to him of the work I'd seen him do,
His eyes grew big as marbles as a twinkle of pride beamed through.
Here was a lad of honor, proud to play a role in life.
We learn to make a living, out on the range we do things right.

You see we have to wrestle for our daily bread,
Not like our city cousins where work is almost dread.
We'll round up in the morning before the rise of sun,
Then never leave our work until it is all done.

I never heard any foul language, and that was a pleasure, too.
Your children they were learning what they had missed in school.
The years of future ranching you'll leave to teenage hands.
I'm sure there won't be any rustling and no falsified brands.

So thanks to all at the rancher's corral,
Where cowboys and ponies and lassoes with large loops,
With teenagers and children and calves in their places
Painted a picture so perfect...to watch was the greatest.

Now as you gather for that prairie oyster stew,
And whatever else those cooks have arranged for you,
There'll be a one-time stranger out on the highway
Feeling so much better having seen you at work that day.

So early tomorrow morning I can see in my mind's eye
A lively group of cowboys ariding into the prairie sky.
Just gathering another herd of cattle while the work will be the same,
Training your sons and daughters life and respect out on the range.

When Your Wife's on the Line

Dana Connelly

Breeding season was over and we brought the bulls home,
But they were still amorous and didn't wanna be alone.
And with cute yearling heifers hanging over the wire
And winking at Old Charolais, his heart was afire.

With girls to the east and girls to the west,
And that bull's roaming eye, my dad thought it best
To send him to boarding school...or so to speak.
He shipped him to a feedlot where awhile he would keep.

Well, Old Charolais musta been awful angry and sore
At being banished to that jail house, 'cause he weren't like before.
When they went to collect him he tore down the alley
And dad's eyes popped wide as he yelled, "Look out, Sally!"

'Midst feed bunks a cracking and the groan of the gate,
As it pulled at its hinges and it was almost too late.
Dad hollered, "Lure him in the trailer. I'll close in from behind!"
But things happened so quick, he didn't have time...

To unlatch the side door for her escape route.
See, with the bull in behind her she had no way out.
Well it seemed like forever 'fore that side door flew free.
A human cannonball shot out, almost too quick to see.

And as she gasped for air and clutched at her heart,
Dad shifted his eyes and waited for her to start.
"What the hell were you thinking!" She looked white as death.
As dad hung his head down and said 'neath his breath,

"I thought ya had it open. Or maybe I forgot.
I just didn't check if it was unlatched or not.
When Old Charolais came charging, it just didn't seem cool
To waste time with checking. Hell, I ain't no fool!

"I hadda get that gate closed, he'd go in but once.
I knew if we lost him we'd be outta luck.
I didn't think he would hurt you, he's all show, can't you see?
And judging the circumstance I knew there'd be...

"Plenty of time to get up to that door.
And Sal, after all, we've been through this before.
And now that you're out, d'ya see the humor? I do."
That was the last straw. I tell you, she blew!

"You think that was funny?! I nearly died!"
And she tore a strip off him a quarter-mile wide.
And I just can't repeat what happened after that,
But I took a lesson and this is a fact.

For you newlyweds who haven't learned yet,
There's a moral to the story you shouldn't forget.
Check EVERYTHING twice and watch your behind,
And DON'T ASSUME ANYTHING when your wife's on the line!

Early Range Riders

George Roberts

Some old cowboys that I used to know
Were quite handy with a rope or gun.
They rode the range many years ago,
That's when the West was fairly young.

Their days of work were hard and long
But they were at home up in the saddle.
They liked a horse both true and strong
Yet the bad ones, they would straddle.

Then there was still some open range,
Though coming fast was the cursed barb wire.
All knew their lives would have to change
That was the topic around any campfire.

On a round-up they got up with the sun,
After hot cakes and bacon, it's back to the grind,
Then rope and brand, till the job was done.
It was their lot so they didn't mind.

Though all were rough and ready.
They took their word and here is why:
Their handshake was firm and steady
And they looked you straight in the eye.

The camaraderie was good as it could be
Among the young and the old boys alike.
But if trouble came you just might see
A real knock-down, all-out fight.

Some of their fights turned into a melee,
As for cuts and bruises, they didn't care.
Still when it was over, you'd likely see
Them shaking hands, much worse for wear.

It wasn't unusual to have pals like that,
Who had big hearts, yet were hard as nails.
They'd give you the shirt right off their back,
Those kind of men blazed the early trails.

Highway 22 North

Pamela Banting

Sunshine over my left shoulder, right hand
relaxed on the wheel, elbow out the window
cultivating a farmer's tan.

In the blue distance a yellow
school bus burps three
ranch kids at their gate.
Screak of door lever,
grind of first, second.

New green greening up.

Ditch grasses hula
with the breezes down there.

                                Dandelions ga-
lore! A yellow lei
swinging with that swaying
                        grass
                            skirt.

Magpie perched on a black cow's back.
Black-white,
                  black-blue, blue-
                              blue,
                              black-black.

Clouds in a pile-up over Water Valley
rolling in like an Old Testament
prophecy, by golly, or Dolly Parton's
hairdo. One or the other.

Hawks atop fence posts, giving every little stirring
their rapt attention. More hawks
preying from on high.

Wing   span.

Honey-dipped palomino grazes pasture land.

Cows also bend
and kiss the earth
chomp, chomp, chomp.

Trucks with horse trailers
like silver bullets,
wait to pull out
from every third side road.
Horses on the move,
caution to the wind.

Horses in the fields are looking good.
Barenaked athletes, muscles
mantled by the sun.

Highway #22.
Northbound.

Motoring.

Seniors of Today

Belle Hall

Let's give praise and lots of love
For our great seniors of today.
They had many trials and tribulations
As they worked from day to day.

They came from families from far-off lands
As children of our great pioneers.
Across the seas and vast open country
To a life, love and fears.

Working together as families should,
Endured many hardships together.
They traveled by horse and buggy or walked many a mile,
A challenge each day in all kinds of weather.

They really didn't know what to expect
As they ventured over the trail.
But faith, hard work and hope,
Their courage and strength would not fail.

Many traveled far and wide
Before they settled down.
Some preferred the country life,
Any many wanted to live in town.

Some made it to the world of fame.
Others weren't quite so lucky.
Seniors of today, rich or poor,
They were certainly very plucky.

The Game Warden
Doug Richards

I was batchin' on a horse ranch.
It was gettin' late on in the fall.
One day the local game warden
Stops in to pay a call.

He says he's out patrollin'
Makin' sure no one commits a sin.
I says, "I'll put the coffee on,
Why don't you come on in?"

While the coffee's boilin'
We proceed to get acquainted.
I begin to think these wardens
Ain't as bad as they been painted.

Well the time it passes quickly.
Next thing we know it's gettin' late.
I says, "You'd better say for supper,
I'll cook us up a bait."

He says, "That sounds good to me
Cause I ain't had no lunch.
Don't make nothing fancy,
But cook up quite a bunch."

I says, "I'll fry some taters
And cook us up some steak,
Heat another pot of coffee,
And some biscuits I will make."

Now we had been a visitin'
Most of the afternoon.
As I start in to cook some supper
Silence invades the room.

So to keep the conversation going,
Cause in manners I'd been coached,
I asked the warden how he like his elk meat,
Roasted, fried or poached.

Reality

Doug Richards

A cowboy stands by his horse
On the edge of some jack pine trees,
Slowly surveying the land he loves,
But not liking all that he sees.

They've called him a jack pine savage
For living so far out in the brush.
But fast cars and good roads have taken him
Within an hour of the downtown rush.

The deeded land all around him
Where once horses and cows did roam,
Is now carved into acreages
And lined with expensive homes.

The wilderness that was his backyard,
Not many people went there.
Now dirt bikes, campers and oil wells
Are scattered everywhere.

In those beaver ponds just below him
He'd always seen moose there before.
Now fishermen stand in the water.
The moose don't come anymore.

He's glad he saw this country
When it was still fresh and new.
He thinks it's all spoiled now,
But there's nothing he can do.

This country was once a horse haven.
There's still a few wild ones out there.
But they and the cowboy are now
Having to learn how to share.

He's thought several times of moving,
But he knows it doesn't make sense.
He's learned the grass ain't greener
Just 'cause it's over the fence.

He doesn't blame folks for coming here;
For them he feels something like pity.
He understands what it must be like
Having to spend your life in the city.

He uses some modern conveniences;
Running water, power and phone.
He has no use for the fast lane
And wishes progress could leave him alone.

Lost in thought, he stands there
In the deepening twilight of gloom,
Knowing full well that progress
Is stealing his elbow room.

Like generations of cowboys before him,
He's had his day in the sun.
But it's in him to be a survivor;
He'll take each change as it comes.

This old world is constantly changing;
It always will, no doubt.
If he doesn't change along with it,
He knows he'll have to die out.

But the cowboy is an adaptable species,
Just like the cockroach and rat.
And you will always find one
Wherever there is space for his hat.

Say a Little Prayer

Sherry Smith

Now I stop and remove my hat,
Step down from the horse where I sat.
With the back of my sleeve, wipe the sweat from my brow.
I figure I better enjoy all of this now.
Boots pointing to the skies,
Sun shining in my eyes,
I lay back in the grass,
As the time does pass.
A fly buzzes around my ear,
As my horse grazes near,
While the pup tugs at the fringe of my chaps,
Thinkin' I'll get up and play perhaps.

A sprig of grass stuck 'tween my teeth.
This chance to relax and reflect, quite a treat.
A rabbit scurries into the brush,
As cattle graze on pasture so lush.
A butterfly flits over the cool, clear creek.
A meadowlark preens its feathers with its beak.
A red fox and her kits frolic in the pasture.
There's the red-tail hawk, I remember from last year.
The breeze tickles my nose
With the scent of wild rose.
A ladybug creeps across my clasped hands.
From a hill, a coyote surveys the land.

Is it all that it seems?
Or is it...just a dream?
Now shaken out of my stupor,
Taken in by all that I view here.
As the puppy licks at my face,
I realize, it is a real place!
So now I close my eyes and whisper a quiet little prayer.
With the encroachment of man...save what becomes rarer and rarer.
The creek quenches a doe and her fawn's thirst,

And I know I'm in the church God created first!
The thought of it all tingles my senses.
As I'm out ridin', all of those fences.

The Ghost Buffalo

Sherry Smith

Eagle Feather rode out alone onto the plain,
From whence many years ago the buffalo came.
In the many thousands they had numbered.
He remembered the hunt that last summer.

Now his people roamed the country, hungry and lost.
Many a child and brave warrior's lives it cost.
He knelt before a rising full moon now in a trance,
With uplifted arms and face, asked the spirits for guidance.

A single eagle feather adorned his headband,
A lonely eagle soared over the shadowed land.
He remembered with honor how he earned that feather,
When buffalo were plentiful and things were better.

Now he sought the spiritual communion in his vision quest.
He changed to the Ghost Buffalo as he knelt to the west,
That white buffalo that in his vision appeared.
He sought contact with it as his memory cleared.

"Where shall I lead my people to find the buffalo herd?"
Only silence, nothing but the soaring eagle stirred.
Then, like a rising mist on the edge of the plain,
The Ghost Buffalo in his vision quest came.

He had sought this vision since the night
The Ghost Buffalo appeared to him so bright.
That night he finally fulfilled his warrior manhood.
The white buffalo spirit appeared as he hoped it would.

He bowed to the ground and thanked the spirits for their guidance.
He was blessed and now his people were saved by the appearance
Of the mighty white buffalo spirit, and now he would know
Where to lead his people, where the buffalo once again roamed.

Mistress
Ron Hodgson

She makes you want her more than you should.
Maybe you should leave, but you know you never could.
She fits in well with your friends, but you need time
When it's just you and her and to heaven you'll climb.

She'll let you caress her whenever you're near.
She smells so sweet and is as soft as cashmere.
She is both beautiful and rugged in her own way,
With an enticing personality that'll make you stay.

When she's angry or upset and she treats you bad,
You will only remember the good times that you've had.
All day she'll cut through to your soul with her icy blade,
Then with one ray of sunshine, her, you will serenade.

She moves from serious to fun without a care,
As she tempts you back, further into her lair.
To be with her makes you want to travel trails
Where you know that danger and risk prevails.

You want her for your own and to be kept for only one,
But she will always be shared just like the rays of the sun.
Don't believe you're her first, neither will you be her only.
A mother she is, and without her, nature would be so lonely.

Saskatchewan

Hi, Dad

Doris Bircham

"Can't I come with you, daddy?"
　　　begs your boy who's just turned three,
as you hoist him onto your shoulders
　　　and bounce him around on your knee.

His eyes and his voice are pleading;
　　　you're sure you know how he feels,
so you take your little boy with you
　　　to the corrals and out to the field.

And you are his dad and his hero,
　　　he hangs on your every word,
and later he tells his mother
　　　the things he's seen and he's heard.

Then somewhere along the way
　　　your son lets go of your hand
and you watch him follow the pathway
　　　that leads from a boy to a man.

As yet he can't quite fill your shoes,
　　　though he almost matches your stride.
He rides with you, he works beside you
　　　and your heart fills with fatherly pride.

Then one day he starts to question
　　　some things you say and do.
It's as though a gate's been thrown open
　　　and your son's about to walk through.

The loop that you built starts slipping,
　　　you know there's no holding him back,
'cause your boy is now in his teens
　　　and you have to cut him some slack.

So you watch him ride on without you,
      you work and you pray and you wait,
and one day when the wind is just right
      your son will ride back through that gate.

And you'll find not a whole lot has changed
      since you bounced your boy on your knee.
He'll look up and grin and shout, "Hi, Dad!"
      like he did when he was just three.

When Jake Got Sick

Doris Bircham

Right after a snow when 'twas thirty below,
    Jake got feelin' right down and out.
He had some kind of flu and one thing I knew
    beyond any reasonable doubt,

Chores had to get done and it wouldn't be fun
    with corrals full of feeders on feed.
So snug past my chin I faced into the wind
    to help in this time of great need.

I worked with our son, was kept on the run;
    with him there's no standing around.
I filled pellet pails, helped haul out the bales
    and spread straw on the calves' bedding ground.

In spite of the cold, chores were under control
    when I walked in the house at noon
to find Jake feelin' rough. He said, "I know it's tough
    but I hope to be back at chores soon."

Doc told Jake to rest and he sure did his best,
    just walked from the couch to the table.
With his concentration on health's restoration...
    peel potatoes? He wasn't able.

'Fore he went to see Doc, he ran, never walked;
    worked himself till he's all hide and bone,
but when Doc said, "Stay in!" he turned weaker 'n sin;
    'twas an effort to pick up the phone.

I said, "Jake I'm no fool and I'm losin' my cool,
    though your sickness does cause me sorrow.
But one thing I ask, is do some light tasks,
    like get dinner ready tomorrow."

Well, Jake fried up some steak, put spuds on to bake
    and generally cooked up a feast,
but the old feed truck died and when I got inside
    it was quarter to one at least.

And for sure you can bet Jake was some upset,
    said my dawdlin' had messed up his life.
"Oh please Lord," I prayed, "make him well right away;
    he's startin' to sound like a wife."

Teamwork

Doris Bircham

For more than thirty-odd years now
    Jake and I've been hitched as a team,
and we've carved a few well-worn trails
    in fields both barren and green.

Jake pulls his load sure and steady
    while I'm sometimes fast, sometimes slow.
And he handles all kinds of weather
    while I balk in mud and deep snow.

But most time we pull well together,
    lean into the harness as one.
For when we turn from each other
    sure enough, a trace comes undone.

Then our load becomes extra heavy
    with each of us fighting the bit,
and it takes a firm tug on the lines
    before either of us will admit...

We need to ease back on our haunches,
    pause awhile, then pull up the slack.
'Cause when our load pushes uphill
    there's no stopping, no turning back.

With calm winds and a load that is light
    there's not too much to upset.
The challenge is climbing steep hills
    when our collars are ringed with sweat.

Where trails are narrow and full of holes
    and rocks are hurting our feet,
some encouragement from our driver
    is sometimes all that we need.

Of course we often wear blinders
    that keep us both looking ahead,
but lately as we jog along
    we glance off to the sides instead.

And we're noticing greener pastures,
    horses standing beside the road
and we know the time is approaching
    when we'll no longer pull our load.

We hope we'll end up in a pasture
    with good grass, clear water to drink,
Side by side we'll lean over the fence
    realizing that we're on the brink

Of making that last long trip out.
    When or how no one can explain.
We only hope we both get to meet
    the One who's been holding the reins.

He Knows

Arlene Boisjoli

The wind blows through the valley.
The cattle chew off the grass.
The sky begins to darken.
Lately the rain just seems to pass.

The calves aren't all that shiny.
Last year they sure were clean.
The rain kept them washed off,
Gave them that healthy sheen.

You know living a long way from town,
Sunday morning just comes and goes.
Church isn't attended often.
Sometimes I wonder if He knows...

That we are good decent people
Who often talk to Him.
That we are thankful for small things.
Get by when pickin's are slim.

When the calf finally starts sucking,
Or the mare that has foaled by herself,
The good beef we raised in the freezer,
Jars of pickles and fruit on the shelf.

The fresh bread baked this morning
Turned out perfect, the family's so proud.
The first sign of the new crop,
The smell of the soil after its plowed.

The peaceful summer evenings,
Frogs croaking in the nearby slough.
Wild flowers scattered over the meadow,
Coyote pups yapping with nothing better to do.

The rhythm of rain on a tin roof
Steadily soaking the ground.
The unbelievable smell the next morning,
The answer is there to be found.

Of course he listens to us.
Look at all the signs everyday.
He doesn't have to speak to me loudly.
Just the rain is enough to say,

He's there, He listens and He knows.

Just Another Poem

Arlene Boisjoli

How do you tell a poem
To a rancher who's wrinkled and old?
How do you tell a story
When the story's already been told?

The wrecks that happen while horseback
Already happened to him.
Gathering in the early morning
When the light was mighty dim.

Feeding in the winter,
When the snow was three feet deep.
Being so darned worried
About the cattle, he couldn't sleep.

Calving in a blizzard,
Cows dropping 'em out on the ground.
Thawing newborns in the bathtub,
Thankful for the live ones found.

Watching the clouds drift over
When he's steadily prayed for rain.
Seeing the barley shrivel,
Not making the grade again.

Cattle prices dropping
Faster then he's ever seen.
Making expenses this year
Will be tricky, the check is lean.

So how do you tell a poem
To a rancher that carries this load?
You just sit back quietly and listen
As his life story begins to unfold.

Grassland Bounty

Harvey Mawson

Between past and future
Is a place called Right Now,
Where survivors still strive
In the land of the cow.
They are the people
Who ride for the brand.
They gather their strength
From the sky and the land.
It's a gift they inherit
To help them keep pace
And to greet each new day
With country-bred grace.

Life is a hound dog
That runs till it dies
Rolling in cow pies
And snapping at flies.
Work is a Phoenix
That flies to the sun,
Rising up from hot ashes
It's time never done.
There is no Pegasus,
Only horses that run
Fading into the distance
In a race never won.
There are no saints,
Only people who try.
Come trial and tribulation
Their faith will not die.

Where badlands nourish only
The hardiest of seed
Grows the grand tradition
Of their ways and their creed.
Rain is their lifeblood,

Their clock is the sun.
By the sweat of their labor
Grassland bounty is won.
They gather their strength
From the sky and the land.
They are the people
Who ride for the brand.

Where I Want to Be

Harvey Mawson

We all have our favorite places,
And for me it's best of all
To be riding on Round Prairie
When they roundup in the fall.

When the days are sunny,
And dawn breaks clear and cold,
The poplars seem to shiver
In their cloaks of molten gold.

The junipers stand like sentinels
On escarpments of brown hills,
And in the river sandbar, serpents
Make restless, rippling rills.

A golden eagle watches
As he spirals up the sky.
Mule deer in a coulee
Near a seep that's never dry.

All of nature's creatures
Are lazy and content,
Without regret for summer days,
Busy and well spent.

Wild geese flock together
To gabble on the lakes,
And cherry leaves turn crimson
Along the edges of the breaks.

Cattle graze the sweet grass
Under cloudless, azure sky.
From the shadowed distance
Haunting, comes a coyote's cry.

Good hands ride the circle
To chase the gather in.
There's magic in the moments
That make a rider grin.

Horse hooves sound a drum beat
To the rhythm of my heart.
Night time brings refreshment,
And each new day a brand new start.

I hear a cowboy whistling
Near the end of the day.
There's satisfaction in the melody
Far greater than his pay.

Calves bawl their confusion,
Wild music rides the breeze,
And a flood tide of future beef
Comes bursting from the trees.

A herd of bovine mothers
Stirs dust along the trail.
Memories come of bygone days,
It never seems to fail.

When experience stirs emotions
That a cowboy's bound to know,
Then feelings dwell in his yearning heart
Wherever he may go.

In this old world there's mystery,
And wondrous things to see;
But when they roundup on Round Prairie
That's where I want to be.

Barb-Wire Vault

Anne Slade

When we had been wed, just a short time, he said,
"Now Honey, here's a good job for you.
While I'm away, check those heifers each day,
there's one of them overdue."

I beamed with pride, though nervous inside
this city gal could finally show
that she could fit in, so keen to begin,
I waved as I watched him go.

That very first day, I went out right away,
checking heifers who weren't even cross.
Why they didn't mind when I viewed their behinds
and I figured that I was the boss.

But I wasn't, I'm confessin', I learned my lesson
and honestly, this is no yarn,
one heifer was complainin', she seemed to be strainin',
so I chased her towards the barn.

She didn't want to go, but how could I know
her water broke when she stood up.
She sniffed the air, like she smelled calf somewhere,
and here's where I ran out of luck.

She turned around, kinda pawin' the ground,
and I didn't think it my place
to stay where I was, so I took off because
I didn't like the look on her face.

I raced for the fence, though that didn't make much sense
'cause heifers run faster than me.
I shoulda jumped higher, but I hit the top wire,
caught my jeans just above the knee.

So I'm hangin' down with my head on the ground
and her snotty nose in my face.
Cow shit in my hair and my boots in the air,
oh gawd, what an awful disgrace!

She huffed and snorted and kinda cavorted,
like she was playin' with me.
She'd back up and stare but she was right there
when I'd reach for that barb in my knee.

Her tail was a mess and I woulda' cared less,
'cept she used it to ward off the flies.
And pieces of crud, mixed in with wet mud
speckled my nose and my eyes.

I hung from the wire, until she got tired
and moved off towards the trees,
then I disconnected, before she objected,
thankful to finally be freed.

When I got in that night, I thought over my plight
and I knew that I was at fault.
My green misreadin's what sent her stampedin'
and taught me the barb-wire vault.

Cowboy Wake

Anne Slade

"Now lass," he said, from his hospital bed,
"You'll do what I ask, I can tell.
Before I'm laid to rest, take a case of the best
to my room at the Cactus Hotel.

"There's no fences to mend with my old friends
though no doubt they've a thirst to slake.
Wipe those tears from your eyes, kiss this old man good-bye
and look after those plans for my wake."

Then just before dawn, they told her he'd gone
and she wasted no time with tears.
She called up the hands who'd helped rope and brand
with her grandfather over the years.

The word traveled far, that they'd set up a bar
in his room at the Cactus Hotel.
His pals drifted in and joined with his kin
to bid the old wrangler farewell.

Recallin' the past, they'd raise up a glass
to their friend laid out by the bed.
Then singin' his praise, they'd toast the old days
recountin' the wise words he'd said.

How in his rough way, he'd taken each day
as a gift to enjoy and share.
And though he was gone, they each carried on
as if the old man was still there.

They'd talk man to man and pat the cold hand
of their pardner laid out with pride.
Sing cowpunchin' songs, to help him along
on his trek cross the Great Divide.

And so for his sake, cowhands at the wake
heeded the things he had asked.
For three days and nights, some sober, some tight,
they reminisced right to the last.

They carried him down, to the main street in town
mounted horse, and rode abreast
of the horse-drawn hearse, to the small country church
where they laid their old friend to rest.

The Favored Hand

Phyllis Kozroski

Tex said he needed Sunday off
and without much hesitation
the boss said, "Sure go right ahead.
Bill can do the irrigation."

Though Bill had plans for Sunday,
when he got home nearin' dawn,
he put away his dancin' boots
pulled knee-high gumboots on.

Tex required a small advance,
the boss promptly cut a check.
When Bill said he was runnin' low
why the bossman gave him heck!

Said careful money management
should be the hallmark of a man.
If he hoped to advance in life
he'd need a sound financial plan.

The boss, he holds his temper
when Tex has a little wreck.
But when it's Bill that's in the soup,
the boss seems to disconnect.

He questions where Bill's mind has gone,
how on earth he's lived this long
without a shred of common sense,
wonders where Bill's mom went wrong!

If Tex thinks up a better plan,
the boss thanks him for the suggestion.
But let Bill offer a new idea
and the odds are quick rejection!

"We've always done the job this way,
don't require much rumination.
It's worked out fine for thirty years,
so we don't need innovation!"

Yep, the boss sure treats 'em different,
but then Tex is the man he hired.
Bill's the one his dreams hitch on,
'cause Bill's the one he sired!

City Cowboy

Phyllis Kozroski

My nephew from the city spent the summer on the ranch.
He'd yearned to be a cowboy, and thought this'd be his chance.
He stayed out in the bunkhouse, that's what real punchers do.
He learned to play some poker, and to spit and swear and chew.

My sis would not be happy with the habits he acquired,
But set on punchin' cows, he trailed the guys we'd hired.
He tried his luck on Sunday, staying on a rank, old steer.
The guys had helped him out some, gave him pointers and some gear.

He didn't last eight seconds, tell the truth, not even four,
But it took the doc ten stitches, or maybe even more.
He said, "Don't worry 'bout the scar, my ma, she won't be stressed.
It makes me look more western, it's a cowboy IQ test!"

He tried his skill at ropin', went and dallied up his thumb.
I hoped the cast'd slow him down, cool his cowboy fever some.
He tried one-handed milkin', said he saw it on TV.
Should've had instruction, Angus ain't a dairy breed.

Scared to call my sister, I tried to think up a good fib,
'Cause he got a concussion, bruises and a broken rib.
His luck seemed to desert him, if to cowboy was his goal.
Sprained his ankle in the pasture, steppin' in a gopher hole.

The old boss cow trampled him; he got too close to her calf.
I hoped he'd notice soon a cowboy's life ain't fun by half.
He slipped right off the hay rack, a bale landed on his chest.
The guy kept right on pickin' to give him a little rest.

He hung in there for weeks and weeks; it really made me tense.
He finally packed it in the day he peed on the 'lectric fence!

107

Cowboy Blessing

Anne Slade

May the rains fall on your pastures
and the grass grow belly high.
May your calves get fat and sassy
and none of your cows be dry.
May your horse be sure-footed
and blessed with good cow sense.
May your neighbors lend a hand
when it's time to mend the fence.
May the sun shine on your crops
when you harvest in the fall.
May your handshake be considered
your word by one and all.
When you life is filled with happiness
or when it's sad and gray,
May those you love be with you
to share each blessed day.

British Columbia

Dylan's Candle

Mike Puhallo

I'm burning Dylan's candle
    and the Welshman didn't lie.
There's a force that drives a poet
    that he simply can't deny.
Sleep is driven from my thoughts
    when the urge is on to write.
Unaware of time or place,
    I scribble through the night.
Forgotten words and passions
    tumble from my pen.
Welling somewhere from within,
    I know not how or when.
Sweet memories and dreams
    dance across the page,
Of carefree youth spent in
    those hills of bunch grass, pine and sage.
I write though I'm exhausted.
    If I try to stand I fall.
Enslaved by the pen
    till the tale will end,
I'm immune to Morpheus' call.

The Man in the Moon

Mike Puhallo

I laid on my back in the cool, damp grass,
about an hour or more,
Just beyond the light of the coal-oil lamp
that shone through the bunkhouse door.

Old Drake came by,
nearly tripped on me and asked,
"Mikey, what are you doin'?"
I said, "Hush up, Jack, and sit a spell.
I'm waitin' for the man in the moon!"
You see, I had my radio there
an' history was in the makin'.
There were things goin' on in the clear night sky
that would set your head to shakin'.

A few at a time, the rest of the crew came out to join us there,
Till ten cowboys lay in the cool, damp grass
and stared up through the clear night air.

Now that old transistor crackled with static,
At times it was damned hard to hear.
But the rising moon was so big and bright
I'd never seen it so near.

Now them folks on the radio chattered on so
about this lunar landing,
an' most of it was technical junk
Beyond my understanding.
Then we heard that spaceman say something
about one small step for a man.
We all hung in close to the radio
to listen the best we can.
Now a lot that broadcast was lost to us
Between static and the coyotes' tune.
But we caught enough to know darn well
A man was on the moon.

113

Now a cowboy can't stay up that late,
the morning comes too soon.
So we drank to his health and each in turn
said "Good night" to the man in the moon.
But it must have been late when I found my bunk,
I slept till nearly four.
And it was my turn to jingle the horses
and knock on the old cook's door.

By the time I had the jingle done
and ran those ponies in,
Dawn was breakin' in the eastern sky
and the moon was pale and thin.
No time to think of spacemen now,
just grab breakfast and leave on a trot.
There's a gather to make and cows to move
before the sun gets hot.

A lot of summers have come and gone
since that one at Douglas Lake.
But none that did so much to mold
the kind of man I'd make.
It was a season full of adventure,
there's lots of memories there.
Like when Darwin's horse pitched him in the creek,
Or the time Red roped the bear.
But by far my fondest memory of a summer that
ended too soon
Was ten cowboys sprawled in the cool, damp grass
Jes' watchin' the man in the moon.

The Story of Montana Slim (Wilf Carter)
(Song)
Shirley Field

He was born in Guysborough, Nova Scotia
Just a quiet, little town in the east.
It was the time of the traveling Chatauqua,
He heard a singing yodeling piece.
It was then that he got the notion
To be a yodeling cowboy too.
At his time was a great commotion
And Slim ended up feeling blue.
He yodeled his way from the upstairs
Out to the old, narrow lane.
His family with all their worries and cares
Thought he was completely insane.
Soon to Calgary, Montana Slim was bound
To work on that good western soil.
And there he started looking around
For some prairie wool to coil.
We watched the cowboys riding down the trail
To round up those broncs for use.
It seemed that they would never fail
When out after an ornery cayuse.
Now Slim never had any trouble
When he was making his pay.
The others knew he was their double
When they were out rounding up strays.
Said Slim, "I ain't no high faluting cowhand,
I reckon just an old cowpoke."
At the Calgary Stampede from the grandstand
Folks watched as his old lasso spoke.
He eared down broncs for a wild-horse race
For the old chuckwagon he outrode.
If he only knew he set the pace
For our cowboys on the open road.
Slim yodeled down trails in the Rockies
Across valleys, among mountain peaks,

Through passes and gaps, on through the trees,
And of his adventures he often speaks.
We all like Slim's singing and yodeling
But Slim's not really his name.
Now I'll tell all you folks, who of this story I bring...
He's Wilf Carter of rodeo and radio fame.
(Yodel)

An Oldtimer's Lament

Jake Conkin

We all used to work together
To help each neighbor out.
Those days have bin a changin'
Till a rancher's future's in doubt.

Brandin', hayin' , 'n puttin' up ice,
Cuttin' 'n haulin' wood, too,
Seems everyone's hurryin' to go nowhere,
Like they's got somethin' important to do.

There ain't time to be neighborly no more.
Everybody's too busy doin' their thing.
Forgettin' to ride with charity in their heart.
"Howdy neighbor" has lost its familiar ring!

Cowboy Medicine

Jake Conkin

Don't be expectin' no fancy doctorin'
Out there on the range.
It'll be treatment 'n medicine
Resemblin' somethin' a might strange.

A sawbone's plenty hard to scare up,
Scarcer than a Latin scholar.
If'n ya gets to hurtin' a lot,
Ain't no use t'be makin' a big holler!

Chances are to be pretty slim
That proper fixin's nearby.
It'll be cookie doin' that doctorin',
Makin' a poultice from a warm cow pie!

Packing Her Bags

Frank Gleeson

Now, she's packing her bags and she's leaving tonight
She says I don't understand the wrong from the right.
She said, "Our marriage is shot...there is no hope."
She says, "You'd either be penning a cow or roping a goat."

She gave me a chance and I failed every test.
Now she's on that old Greyhound and she's heading west.
She says she's not going to stop 'til she gets to the sea,
And she'll sit on the sand and the beach without me.

She says, "You're out playing cowboy at my expense
I'm home, either nursing a calf or fixing a fence."
So cowboy be careful with that little gal.
Come on admit it, she's probably your very best pal.

'Cause that's the same little gal that's cooking the beans.
And who do you turn to, to patch up your jeans?
'Cause she may not be interested in how fast you roped that steer,
Or how long it takes you to drink up your beer.

She may have a different idea that she calls fun.
Better listen real closely or soon she'll be gone.
Now she doesn't mind you cowboying once in a while,
But every darn night is just cramping her style.

So cowboys change your ways for the sake of your girlfriend or wife,
'Cause she might leave you for the rest of your life.
She might leave and never come back,
And I'll bet you'll miss this little gal of yours in the sack.

So spend some time with her for both of your sakes.
Lay off the cowboying for a day, take her out to the lake.
Take her to a movie and wine and all that.
Then you can go back roping for a week and pulling your slack.

Then you'll grow old together, bind your vows real tight.
Respect each other's freedom, and you'll never fight.
Now that's the code of the West, to live brave and free,
To respect each other's rights and that's the way it should be.

The Environment

Frank Gleeson

The other night, I arrived home late
And there was this van parked down by my gate.
The environmentalists were there; they were chanting their song
Saying I was doing just about everything wrong.

They said I was cutting down too many trees to make room for the hay.
I was wasting too much water on irrigation spray,
Pumping far too much water just to grow grass
And my cows were letting out far too much gas.

They said I was ruining the water for humans to drink
And they said my old milk cow was starting to stink.
Now I have to admit, although it was late,
There was a pretty strong odor down by the gate.

But a funny thing happened later that day
When them tree huggers left, that smell went away.
They were blaming my cows but they're not in that class.
It's them tree huggers letting out all of that gas.

They want me to put little toilets through the bush,
But how do you teach those old Charolais to flush?
I could put all the calves in a neat little diaper
And give all the cows a big roll of paper.

But all jokes aside, we only have one planet.
We have to get along 'cause we have to live on it.
Now that doesn't make me right and the other guy wrong,
But protecting our lifestyle, our feelings are strong.

We don't want special treatment with no fancy frills.
I just want to make a good living and pay all our bills.

Yukon/ Northwest Territories

Andy Bahr

Stu Conner

Our crew of ghostly cowboys stood there hipshot by the Gate,
Discussin' bovine topics and began to speculate.
And pretty soon we hunkered down to do as old hands do;
While some pulled out the makin's, others passed around a chew.

We started tellin' tales of our former earthly days,
Discussin' things like movin' stock and pickin' up the strays.
We somehow got to braggin' on the wondrous things we'd seen
And what the tribulations of them trail drives had been.

Some said Mr. Goodnight was the king of trail drives,
But some said they knew tougher men when they was still alive.
Some did debate the longest trail and some talked of the worst.
And some spoke of the driest drives with which they had been cursed.

T'was some who argued Texas herds was bigger than the rest,
And that the boys who moved 'em out were better than the best.
Wyomin' boys said Texas was a big old piece of cake
That never knowed the winter drives that they was prone to make.

The Colorado cowboys claimed the mountains was the thing
That proved beyond a foolish doubt just who was truly king.
Albertans vowed Saskatchewan was like a nursery,
And B.C. swore Alberta was a picnic, don't you see?

And on it went with desert worse than mountain worse than snow,
And rain and hail and blizzards when the Great Blue Northers blow;
Of runaways and rivers swift, of lightning and poor feed,
Of cooks so purely awful it would make your stomach bleed.

While each man tried to make his case and make it good and strong,
A feller in the strangest set of soogans come along.
He stood, oh, maybe five-foot-four beneath that suit of fur,
You couldn't hardly see his face but we was pretty sure...

That this here gent had strayed off from a herd of Eskimos,
For who else needed furs right from his head down to his toes?
Old Jake said, "Friend, I guess you haven't found your outfit yet.
But if your tired óf searchin', why, ground-hitch yourself and set.

"For any man is welcome, well, unless he was a vet.
But vets and politicians couldn't get here on a bet.
This section is for cowboys but you're likely lathered up,
There's coffee on the fire if you'd care to pour a cup.

"We're just debatin' trail drives (if you know what that is),
And every cow nurse settin' here is claimin' he's a whiz.
Just rest and listen for a while and shuck that fur suit off,
We'll find your outfit by and by, 'cause friend, you're surely lost."

Well no, he said, he wasn't lost, Saint Pete had sent him here.
And though he said he wasn't sure exactly what's a steer,
St. Pete had asked him all about the work he did on Earth,
And when he'd told it all, it seemed to cause no end of mirth.

Pete said, "You tell those cowboys all about your trail drive.
I'd like to be there when you do, to look into their eyes."
He said, "I think you'll fit right in, just tell 'em what you done.
I wish that I could be there, Lord, it surely would be fun!"

Well, you know curiosity a cowboy can't deny.
He wondered what the motives of St. Peter might be.
We thought we better hear his tale to see what we could see,
And partner, we all got a lesson in HUMILITY!

And by and by he said that he was not an Eskimo,
But he'd spent many, many years a herdin' in the snow.
It seems some fancy bureaucrats would save the Eskimo,
And teach 'em herdin' reindeer was the only route to go.

While on a desk in Ottawa, the plan looked mighty slick.
They figured in some extra days for nature and her tricks.
They calculated cans of fruit and toilet paper rolls,
And documented mileage and set out daily goals.

So they allowed him eighteen months; the worst case? Well, two years.
Three thousand head and all prime stocks; no need for foolish fears!
Alaska was the herd's home range, just push them east and north.
If mountains might get in the way, so what? Just carry forth!

Be careful crossing rivers in the long, dark Arctic night,
And when you hit the ocean it's a signal to turn right.
You can't go wrong for there's a map and schedule for each day
And don't forget, no losses are allowed along the way.

Just trot across Alaska and don't dawdle on the way.
Then hurry through the Yukon; maybe rest up half a day.
The Northwest Territories is the last stretch to be found.
You can't miss Kittigazuit, the only pens around.

Now, while he talked it seemed a chill had crept into the air.
We moved into the bunkhouse and pulled up some high-backed chairs.
Then Red pulled out a bottle and we passed it man to man;
We knew that we was hearin' from a man who was a HAND!

Now, any other bunkhouse night was pretty much the same,
A little chore you need to do, then deal a poker game.
Old Gabby would be yarnin' while he rolled a rawhide quirt.
Curly might be makin' elkhorn buttons for his shirt.

Spence would be a-braidin', Charlie splicin' on a rope;
Jed might be a-workin' on some tac with saddle soap.
One might change a latigo or mend some harness straps;
Some might be debatin' shotgun versus batwing chaps.

The thing I want to get at is that every mother's son
Is workin' at a project that he's anxious to get done.
But on the night we heard this tale nobody made a sound.
It seemed at last the world's greatest drover had been found.

Now, I'll not try to fill you in on how he moved that herd,
For when you get here for yourself, you'll hang on every word.
And every single one of you should open up your ears.
You'll learn about a trail drive that lasted five long years.

So when your earthly ridin's done and you retire up here,
Come meet an Arctic cowboy who has trailed three thousand deer.
A little guy from Lapland with a funny set of clothes;
We've got him in our bunkhouse; he's still thawin' out his toes.

Another Tall Bear Tale

Jim Green

Colin Hedderick told dad about the time
He and his partner stumbled onto a bear.
It charged, Colin ran, then tripped,
Dropped his rifle and kept running,
Running round and round and round
A runty little clump of scrub willow.

The partner got hisself all in lather,
Being somewhat new to bear country doings.
So every time the two of 'em come around
He'd jack another cartridge outta his rifle.
No shooting, mind you,
Just jack another full round out into the crisp fall air.

About the fifth or sixth go-round,
Hedderick was getting just a tad winded.
So he hollered instructions to buddy,
"You run for awhile and I'll shoot."
So that's what they done, his partner took the relay,
Hedderick shot the bear.

Dad had his doubts about it at first, too.
But Colin had the hide on the cabin floor.
A full head mount, including the teeth,
That dad stumbled over on midnight trips
To the outside biffy...so what the heck,
With that kind of proof, it had to be true.

I Didn't Cheat, Said Rattlesnake Pete

Jim Green

Jesse Hinman and Rattlesnake Pete
Was playing cards in Pincher Creek.
And when a gentle altercation arose,
One hit the other smack on the nose.

Jesse drew like lightning so fast,
Let fly at Pete a thunderous blast.
But the shot missed, Pete weren't dead,
So Jesse tried to bust open his head.

The trial itself, it didn't take long.
Jesse swore, then he sang his sad song.
But the judge, he shore give him the gears,
Sent old Jesse down for five long years.

Montana

Cabin Fever

Bob Ross

Clem and me is batchin'
    Over on the Musselshell.
We both have cabin fever
    And it is cold as hell.
The cattle's brushed up in the willers
    And a hump is in their backs.
The cottonwoods is poppin'
    With a sound like rifle cracks.

For days the wind's been from the north
    And the snow is piled up deep.
The blizzard keeps a ragin'
    Till we hear it in our sleep.
We chop the ice and scatter "cake"
    And try to keep from freezin',
But this cabin fever pard of mine
    Is anything but pleasin'.

Holed up in this line shack
    Which is only 12 by 10
Makes pretty crowded quarters
    Fer me and Clem.
Our deck of cards I plumb worn out
    From playin' solitaire.
A Chinook would be a welcome sight
    To bring some warm spring air.

Clem's a little "light upstairs"
    And kinda "loosely wrapped."
He talks a steady stream of nonsense
    'Till my patience's nearly snapped.
He talks about the weather
    And all the girls he's knowed,
The ranchers that he's worked for
    And the horses he has rode.

We tell each other whoppers
    'Bout rattlesnakes and things
And argue over scorpions
    And if they bite or sting.
He prattles on from dawn till dark
    And far into the night,
Then he starts in again
    As soon as it is light.

Clem hasn't had no learnin'
    'Cept the school of hard knocks,
But he shore knows cows and horses
    And he is crazy like a fox.
He seems to have a special sense
    Though he can hardly read or write
And, it gripes me when we argue
    'Cause Clem's nearly always right.

I learned survival tricks from Clem
    To combat winter scenes.
Like a bag of shavings in my coat
    Soaked in kerosene;
Or a paper sack o'er my boot
    Inside my overshoe.
But he'd rattle on and rant and rave
    Always with his point of view.

He showed me how to braid rawhide
    And make a hackamore,
How to braid with many strands
    Eight, six or four.
His braid work is beautiful
    Be it flat, round or square.
He seems to have a special touch
    With a most artistic flair.

He shore kin cook a pot of beans
    Either red or white,
But those everlasting lies of his

Just make me want to fight.
I guess he never really lies,
        Clem's done a lot of things.
The fact he seldom lets me talk
        Is the part that really stings.

Clem's bakin' powder biscuits
        I scorn with every bite.
They are always real tasty
        And turn out fluffy light.
You know I'm so doggone jealous
        I think I'll hide the cleaver.
No tellin' what might happen
        Till we cure this cabin fever.

Long-Legged Cowpuncher

Bob Ross

I knowed an old-time cowboy
    Who went by the name of Jim.
I'd like to share with you a story
    I once heard from him.
Now, Jim's a gettin' agey
    And kinda long in the tooth,
But he's usually fairly honest
    And nearly always tells the truth.

Jim sez, "One day I'm ridin' fence
    On a bronc that's prone to buck,
But we'll make it back to camp by dark
    With a little bit of luck.
The country that I'm ridin' in
    Is really mighty rough,
But that was way back years ago
    When cowboys was all tough.

"The fence drops off a rugged ridge
    As steep as an old cow's face.
Right then a rattler buzzes down under us
    And my cayuse changed his pace.
He exploded like a time bomb
    And me with no defense.
I went ten feet up in the air
    And lit astride a fence.

"I slid down the top barbed wire
    And busted off two posts,
But grabbed aholt that third fence post
    And stopped that dreadful coast.
I thought I'd hit a buzz saw
    That ripped me most in two,
But cowboys aren't resourceful
    And do what they have to do.

"Here I am ten miles from camp
     And I'm in quite a quander,
I'm ripped clear up to my belt line
     And my legs are somewhat longer."
Then Jim just stopped in his story tellin'
     And started to roll a smoke.
I waited a couple of minutes
     Before I ever spoke.
I sez, "What'd you do then, Jim
     That must've ruffled yer feathers?"
"Naw," he sez, "I just caught my horse standin' there
     And let out the stirrup leathers."

The Final Tally

Now this book is all done
And you've had some fun
Reading poems of life and good times.
Cowboy poetry is here
To stay, that is clear
So on with our gatherings, rambles and rhymes.
                    Susan Ames Vogelaar

Biographies

Pamela Banting

Pamela was born and raised in Birch River in the Swan River Valley, Manitoba, and is currently living in Calgary, Alberta. She has published two books, *Running into the Open* and *Bareback*. Her work has also been published in numerous other anthologies. Pamela's poetry explores her feelings for the land and nature and the difficulty of living in the city after being raised with the solace of open spaces.

Rose Bibby

Rose makes her home in Westlock, Alberta, with her husband Garth. They perform her poetry at banquets, conferences and poetry gatherings where Rose tells how it happens and Garth tells how it really is. Rose is the author of *Rosebrair Ranch Ramblings*, *Rosie Rambles On* and *Rosie's Rhyme and Reason*. Their tapes include *Hayshakers "Live" at the Bluff* and *Hayshakers "Live" at the Bluff 2*.

Doris Bircham

Doris and her husband Ralph ranch on Bear Creek in the Cypress Hills in Saskatchewan. Her poetry reflects daily family life on the ranch. She has been helping organize the annual Maple Creek Gathering since its beginning. Her publications include *Calving and the Afterbirth*, and *Pastures, Ponies and Pals*. Together with coauthor Anne Slade, she has produced two tapes *Prairie Wool* and *Pastures, Ponies and Pals* as well a children's calendar, *Kids' Country Calendar*.

Arlene Boisjoli

Arlene lives with her husband and four children on a ranch along the South Saskatchewan River near Glidden. Her experience of ranching in Alberta and Saskatchewan has led to a love of the lifestyle and a love of the land, which are reflected in her poetry. Arlene helped to organize the Pincher Creek Cowboy Poetry Gathering when she made her home in Willow Valley. She is the author of *Cowboy Hats and Roses* and *Leather, Chaps and Crocuses*.

Don Brestler

Born and raised in Alberta, Don worked as a cowboy, guide, packer and horse wrangler in Waterton Lakes National Park. He has ridden in rodeos and has broken horses at the Ya Ha Tinda Government Horse Ranch. Don is an acclaimed artist, songwriter and musician. He lives with his wife Ingrid in Twin Butte, Alberta.

Leane Buxton

Leane began putting thoughts to rhyme when she wanted to tell folks how she feels about the land, why she chooses to live on it and about the people she has met who make it all worthwhile. She lives on her family homestead in Westlock, Alberta, where she finds daily inspiration in her surroundings and young family.

Jake Conkin
Jake is a British Columbian cowboy poet, storyteller, author, historian and producer of cowboy cultural events including *The Buckaroo Jake Kid's Show*. He is the author of *Silk and Silver*. Jake is presently working on a children's novel, *Little Jake's Cowdog*.

Dana Connelly
Dana grew up on the family ranch on Connelly Creek, Alberta. She comes from a traditional musical background and she writes and sings western music. Dana has performed with Joanne Moody at many gatherings throughout Saskatchewan and Alberta and also enjoys writing cowboy poetry.

Doris Daley
Now living in Calgary, Doris is a native of a southern Alberta ranch country. She has published *The Daley Grind*, a collection of her poems. Doris has been a featured performer at many different functions throughout Western Canada and has performed in Madison, Wisconsin.

Lloyd Dolen
Lloyd and his wife Norma live on their ranch near Cochrane, Alberta. Lloyd celebrated his 80th birthday in February, 1997, and he has been writing for many years. His experience with rodeo, ranching and raising a family have given him an insight into life which is reflected in his poetry.

Ezra Eberhart:
Ezra still makes his home on his orginal homestead near Holden, Alberta, where he was born. He refers to himself as a "mixed-up farmer" who is involved in farming, grain and cattle. He has been writing poetry for twenty years.

Shirley Field
Shirley has a wealth of experience in the entertainment industry. She recorded her first single in Nashville, Tennessee, in 1962, appeared on the *Grand Ole Opry* and *The Earnest Tubb Jamboree* and has toured with Marty Robbins. She became the Canadian Female Yodelling Champion and the National Yodelling Champion in Tucson, Arizona. Shirley has been singing country western music for fifty years. She writes songs and poetry and entertains at gatherings, festivals and cattle drives throughout the western provinces and the United States. Armstrong, B.C., is her home.

Bud Gale
Bud was born in Buck Lake, Alberta, in 1928 and now makes his home in Sherwood Park. Bud describes himself as old and ornery, neither of which appears to be true. His poems outline the ranching and rodeo community in the 1930s and 1940s. He shares his stories about the real West at gatherings and special events.

Frank Gleeson

The Lone Birch Ranch in Williams Lake, B.C., is where Frank and Betty Gleeson make their home. Frank raises commercial cattle on his ranch. His poetry reflects the everyday happenings of life as he sees it. Frank's sense of humor shows through as he writes about situations that he gets himself into. He has performed throughout Western Canada and was a feature poet at Pincher Creek, Alberta, and at Elko, Nevada.

Morrie MacIntosh Goetjen

An Alberta native, Morrie and his wife operate the Whisky Ridge Cattle Company near Ardrie, Alberta. Morrie's poetry leans toward the ideosyncracies and frustrations of handling the beloved cow. He enjoys performing at gatherings and other social functions.

Jim Green

Jim grew up in Pincher Creek, the ranching country of Southern Alberta, and now makes his home in Fort Smith, Northwest Territories. He is a western storyteller and poet who leans heavily toward the history of cattle country.

Belle Hall

Of Scottish descent, Belle was born in De Winton and has farmed around Calgary and the Cochrane area all her life. In 1986, she began sharing some of her experiences through writing and reading her poetry.

Ron Hodgson

Ron moved to Calgary from Saskatchewan in the late 1960s and has traveled in the mountains ever since. He started riding and hunting around the Etherington Creek in Southern Alberta, and later in the Hinton and Grande Cache areas as well as Banff and Lake Louise. Ron includes these experiences in his poetry.

Tom Hogarth

Tom's roots are in the Stettler area, where he grew up on a mixed farm. He has been writing and performing traditional western music for the past fifteen years. Tom now makes his home in Calgary, Alberta.

Phyllis Kozroski

Phyllis and her husband, Dennis, ranch in the east end of the Cypress Hills in Saskatchewan. In addition to a cow-calf operation, they run a small feedlot and grow some cereal crops. Phyllis has been performing cowboy poetry since 1993. She is the author and illustrator of *Friends and Neighbors, Tried and True*, a collection of cowboy Christmas cards and a poster, *Pat's Advice*.

Don Marino

Don (alias Stu Conner) was born and raised in southern Alberta in the Lethbridge area. Not being comfortable in a crowd, he moved to the Yukon Territory in 1976 to go trapping and soon after started a hunting outfit. Currently, he is developing a farm near Carmacks, Yukon, is gold mining and is writing poetry when the mood strikes.

Harvey Mawson

A lifetime cowboy, Harvey's roots go back to cattle and horse ranching which his family began in 1882. Harvey makes his home in Dundurn, Saskatchewan. He has performed throughout Western Canada and has appeared at Elko, Nevada. Harvey is the author of *Portraits, Before the Plow, Cowboy Up, Truth, Legend and Lies*, and *Brimstone and Bobwire*. He is presently writing two books, one of short stories and the other a novel.

Alanna Murray

Originally from rural Manitoba, Alanna now lives on a ranch near Kathryn, Alberta. Her rural experiences have given her a wealth of material for her poetry. Alanna has published one book entitled, *Thinking Outloud*.

Rob Osberg

Rob and his wife Diane live on a ranchette near Bragg Creek. Pack trips through the mountains are a favorite hobby of Rob's. Many of his poems reflect the cowboy's gentler side and his appreciation of the natural environment. Rob is the author of *Magpie Tales* and he has published a tape of the same name.

Mike Puhallo

Mike is a partner in a cattle ranch and a trucker as well as an artist and cowboy poet. Mike was on the rodeo circuit for twenty years starting at the age of sixteen. He makes his home near Kamloops, B.C. Mike has coauthored three books, *Rhymes on the Range, Still Rhymin' on the Range* and *Can't Stop Rhymin' on the Range*.

Doug Richards

Doug was born and raised on the Devil's Head Ranch in the foothills west of Cochrane, Alberta, which he and his family now operate. Being raised on an isolated, pioneer ranch, Doug acquired his education through correspondence, 4H and the experiences of day-to-day ranching. Much of his work is humorous and shows the lighter side of life.

George Roberts

Born in 1907, George is a former cowboy, rodeo contestant, boxer and is still a writer. He worked at the Buffalo Hills Ranch for fourteen years. George has been sharing his poetry with audiences for several years. He has published two books, *Looking Back* and *Buffalo Chips and Prairie Grass*. George makes his home near Arrowwood, Alberta.

James Roberts

One of the younger poets in the ACPA, James began reciting at eighteen. He was born in Pincher Creek and raised in Valleyview. He worked as a cowboy on a community pasture at Manning and another at Valleyview. He is presently attending university in B.C. and has plans to enter RCMP training.

Staff Sergeant W. J. "Robbie" Robertson (Ret'd.)
Robbie was associated with the RCMP for a period of forty years. He writes poetry about the early history of the force and some of its heroes. Dressed in his period red serge, Robbie recites his own poetry and traditional poems at gatherings which have included far away places like London, England, and Texas.

Bob Ross
Born and raised in the Bull Mountains of South Central Montana, Bob now makes his home in Bozeman, Montana. He was a combat infantryman in World War II. Bob has been writing poetry for thirty-five years and he has published four poetry books.

Christine Schauer
Christine was born and raised in Millet, Alberta. She now makes her home in Sundre, Alberta, along the James River. She has been writing music, songs and poetry since the 1980s.

Anne Slade
A ranch in the Cypress Hills near Tompkins, Saskatchewan, is where Anne calls home. Adjustment to life on the ranch and an interest in rural people and their history has provided material for some of her poems. Anne writes for both adults and children and as well as performing, she presents poetry workshops. She has authored, *Denim, Felt & Leather* and with Doris Bircham she coauthored *Pastures, Ponies and Pals* as well as a tape of the same name.

B. J. Smith
Raised in Wyoming on a hereford ranch, working for Sandy Cross at the Rothney Farms and now ranching with her husband and six children just north of Edmonton raising Simmental cattle, has given B. J. a wealth of material for her poetry. She has been writing since she was a child and now performs her work at gatherings and special events.

Sherry Smith
Thorhild, Alberta is Sherry's home. She works parttime as a general aide in the senior's lodge and the rest of her time is spent training horses as well as riding her own quarter horse gelding. She writes about her love of nature and her appreciation of the rural lifestyle.

Bryn Thiessen
The author of *Wind in the Pines*, Bryn has written poetry and performed throughout Western Canada. He brings a unique style to the presentation of his work. He is the president of the Alberta Cowboy Poetry Association and makes his home on Helmer Creek Ranch near Sundre, Alberta.

Darryl Vance

With his wife, Judy, and his children, Darryl ranches on his Grassy Butte place south of Pincher Creek, Alberta. He has been a brand inspector for years and is well known in the area. He plays piano and guitar and has also acted in a local drama club. Darryl began performing at the Pincher Creek Gathering and now shares his music and poetry at different events throughout Alberta.

Susan Vogelaar

A native of Pincher Creek, Alberta, Susan has spent the past twenty-nine years raising her three children on a spread east of Pincher Creek with her husband. The daily experiences of living the rural lifestyle, raising children, cattle, horses, dogs and other creatures, provide countless experiences that often find their way into her poems. She has two self-published poetry books, *Whistling in the Wind* and *Musings from the Outhouse*. Susan travels to many gatherings and festivals sharing her poetry with those who come to listen.

Wendy Vaughan

Raised on a cattle and horse ranch in the Ghost River area thirty miles west of Cochrane, Alberta, Wendy received her education at home until grade 12. She presently resides with her husband and two daughters on their cattle farm north of Cochrane. Her first book, soon to be released, is titled *The Corral Bars are Down*.

Bill Wearmouth

Bill passed away in March, 1997. Bill's roots were in Cochrane, Alberta where he grew up during the Great Depression. He began farming and competing in rodeos and then began a demolition contracting business that became "Wearmouth Canada Inc." With his wife Carla, they raised nine children and have fifteen grandchildren. Bill was always a country boy at heart and enjoyed writing and performing poetry. He will be missed by his friends and fellow poets.

Irene Wert

Star City, Saskatchewan, was Irene's birthplace. She has written poetry most of her life. Writing and performing cowboy poetry has made her senior years rewarding as she makes new friends and travels to gatherings and other social functions. Irene now makes her home in Leduc, Alberta.

Dixie Lee White

Dixie is the secretary/treasurer of the Alberta Cowboy Poetry Association. She makes her home on a ranch west of Claresholm, Alberta. George and Dixie own the Rustler Rope Company as well as sport stock. Dixie has been writing and reading her poetry for two years.

Index